CREATIVE
CODING

Lessons and Strategies to Teach Computer Science Across the 6-8 Curriculum

JOSH CALDWELL

International Society for Technology in Education

PORTLAND, OREGON • ARLINGTON, VIRGINIA

Creative Coding

Lessons and Strategies to Teach Computer Science Across the 6-8 Curriculum

Josh Caldwell

© 2018 International Society for Technology in Education

World rights reserved. No part of this book may be reproduced or transmitted in any form or by any means—electronic, mechanical, photocopying, recording, or by any information storage or retrieval system—without prior written permission from the publisher. Contact Permissions Editor: iste.org/about/permissions-and-reprints; permissions@iste.org; fax: 1.541.302.3780.

Editor: *Emily Reed*
Copy Editor: *Karstin Painter*
Proofreader: *Corinne Gould*
Book Design and Production: *Jeff Puda*
Cover Design: *Edwin Ouellette*

Library of Congress Cataloging-in-Publication Data
Names: Caldwell, Josh (Curriculum developer), author.
Title: Creative coding : lessons and strategies to teach computer science
  across the 6-8 curriculum / Josh Caldwell.
Description: First edition. | Portland, Oregon : International Society for
  Technology in Education, [2018] | Includes bibliographical references. |
  Identifiers: LCCN 2018016641 (print) | LCCN 2018020751 (ebook) | ISBN
  9781564846730 (mobi) | ISBN 9781564846747 (epub) | ISBN 9781564846754 (
  pdf) | ISBN 9781564846761 (pbk.)
Subjects: LCSH: Computer science–Study and teaching (Middle school)
Classification: LCC QA76.27 (ebook) | LCC QA76.27 .C34 2018 (print) | DDC
  004.071/2–dc23
LC record available at https://lccn.loc.gov/2018016641

First Edition
ISBN: 978-1-56484-676-1
Ebook version available.

Printed in the United States of America.

ISTE® is a registered trademark of the International Society for Technology in Education.

MIX
Paper from responsible sources
FSC www.fsc.org FSC® C008955

About ISTE

The International Society for Technology in Education (ISTE) is the premier non-profit organization serving educators and education leaders committed to empowering connected learners in a connected world. ISTE serves more than 100,000 education stakeholders throughout the world.

ISTE's innovative offerings include the ISTE Conference & Expo, one of the biggest, most comprehensive ed tech events in the world—as well as the widely adopted ISTE Standards for learning, teaching and leading in the digital age and a robust suite of professional learning resources, including webinars, online courses, consulting services for schools and districts, books, and peer-reviewed journals and publications. Visit iste.org to learn more.

Join our community of passionate educators!

ISTE members get free year-round professional development opportunities and discounts on ISTE resources and conference registration. Membership also connects you to a network of educators who can instantly help with advice and best practices.

Join or renew your membership today! Visit iste.org/membership or call 800.336.5191.

Also in the Coding and Computational Thinking in the Classroom Series

No Fear Coding: Computational Thinking across the K-12 Curriculum, by Heidi Williams

To see all books available from ISTE, please visit iste.org/resources.

About the Author

 Josh Caldwell leads the curriculum team at Code.org, where he oversees the development of Code.org's entire K-12 path of computer science curriculum courses. In addition to guiding curriculum development, he has run professional learning workshops for teachers across the country, with a particular focus on helping teachers of other content areas to begin teaching computer science. Before joining Code.org, Josh taught middle school outside Seattle, Washington, where he developed a pathway of computer science and robotics courses, in addition to teaching English Language Arts.

Acknowledgments

I have to first give my deepest thanks to my incredible wife, Megan, for her never-ending support as I brought "just one more thing" into our already busy schedule. I want to thank Hadi Partovi and everyone at Code.org, whose support allows me to continue learning and developing my own understanding of computer science education. In particular, I owe much to the educators on the team who challenge me and help me to learn and grow as an educator, including Elizabeth Bacon, Sarah Filman, Baker Franke, Dani Macavoy, Brook Osborne, Kiki Prottsman, GT Wrobel, and Pat Yongpradit. I'd also like to thank Irene Lee and Emmanuel Schanzer, who have been integral to how I think about integrating computer science into science and math, respectively. Finally, thank you to all of the amazing educators that I've had the immense fortune to work with through the workshops I facilitate. Quite frequently, I feel that I learn more from those dedicated teachers who bring their diverse experiences to the room than I could ever hope to return.

To Sue Russell, my teaching mentor. You set me on the path I'm on today, and your guidance continues to keep me responsible to the ones who really matter, the students.

Contents

PART 1 Tools and Strategies

PART 2 Coding in Core Content Areas

Contents

PART 3 Assessment and Feedback

Foreword

Every student—no matter their race, gender, religious or cultural beliefs—should have the opportunity to learn computer science (CS). The basic skills help nurture creativity and problem-solving and can prepare students for future careers. In the past ten years, there has been a huge push for STEM and CS focus areas in education. However, there is still a lack of resources in underrepresented areas and courses offered, and African American and Hispanic women are not still not represented equally in technical fields in the workplace. Diversity has played a huge role in this decline as well. Statistics have shown that there is a lack of women being represented and the culprit stems from school age. In this current day and age, we find that 74% of girls in middle school have a strong interest in STEM and CS fields, but only 4% of them actually major in those fields in college.

In order to change this sobering statistic, there must be a shift in the mindset of who is represented in STEM and CS fields by involving girls at an early age. It starts with educators changing the mindset that CS and STEM are only for select groups of students or those who are gifted and talented. We as educators need to reflect on our own biases as we work to encourage students that they can do and be whatever they would like. Encourage students to dream and strive to be the best in whatever they are passionate about. Allow them to explore various fields, experience real world connections, think outside of the box—better yet, don't even think with a box in mind.

It starts with us: educators! We must become excited about learning and shifting our mindset that computer science is not just for the stereotypical "nerds," but for everyone. Anyone can learn to code! Shift the mindset and come together to discuss why there is a lack of women in this field. How can we be role models? How can we get rid of our own biases of who should or shouldn't be in technology careers? Encourage your students to be whatever they want to be. Let's change who is represented in these field by starting a movement in our classrooms, our communities, and in our homes.

It starts with you, and *Creative Coding* is the perfect tool to get you started on the path of introducing computer science in your classroom. In this book, Josh Caldwell takes the reader through a number of strategies that you can readily use in a classroom, school district, or in the community to address many issues surrounding computer science in middle school. This book is for anyone, no matter your level of computer science knowledge or skillset. Caldwell walks the reader through incorporating computer science in any content area to have it work seamlessly. He shows that incorporating computer science concepts or activities doesn't have to be something extra for your class to do. The book also provides projects, resources, and strategies that are basically plug and play and outstanding as tools to incorporate computer science right away.

Seeing how easy CS is to incorporate can help break those stereotypes that have built up around it. The activities in this book will show you that anyone can code and through CS can learn powerful skills for the future!

Kimberly Lane Clark, Ed.S. is a nationally award-winning educator and speaker based in Texas. Kimberly earned a B.A. in Educational Technology, a M.Ed. in Secondary Education, and an Ed.S. in Secondary Education with a specialization in Educational Technology from Jackson State University. She began her career in educational technology 11 years ago, gaining experience teaching students in grades K–12 in Mississippi and Texas. She coaches hundreds of educators, both face-to-face and virtually, in computer science integration, blended learning strategies, and educational technology. In the latter part of her years in education she also served as a campus technology coordinator. She was selected as the third cohort of the TED-Ed innovators in 2016 and the 2017–2018 ISTE Computer Science Network president. Kimberly is currently a district blended learning specialist in Texas.

Introduction

I came to teaching as a second career. When I first met with my graduate-school adviser, I knew little more than that I enjoyed working with kids, and I enjoyed middle-school students in particular. What I didn't yet know was *what* I wanted to teach, or what I even *could* teach. I had been a theater major in college, but theater positions aren't available frequently.

I'd been working in IT and had done a little coding for both work and pleasure. I thought computer science might be a subject for which I'd have a basic skill set and enjoy teaching, but I was told there was no such thing as a computer science endorsement. Computer science teachers were some sort of mystical entity—the professors in my program knew they existed, but nobody could tell me how to become one. After a fairly long discussion of my skills and interests, and an in-depth review of my college transcripts (I needed enough credits to be considered "highly qualified" in my chosen endorsement), we landed on an English Language Arts (ELA) endorsement.

I loved teaching English, and I like to believe I was pretty good at it. But despite my love for the subject, I had a gnawing voice in the back of my mind. I knew that

Introduction

I had benefited from my experience with computer science. It had changed the way I thought, empowered me to create and solve interesting problems, and it was something I enjoyed, but it wasn't something to which my students had any access. I had the privilege of parents who supported my interests, but access to something as powerful and transformative as computer science shouldn't be predicated on privilege. The students who get access shouldn't be only those whose families can afford expensive coding camps. What's the point of public education if not to ensure that every child enters adulthood equipped with the tools to engage, contribute, and succeed in society? Today, that must mean that students are at least literate in computer science, and if the school district wasn't going to make that happen, then I had to.

Starting with small projects, I incorporated programming and computational thinking into my ELA classes. I started by simply swapping out the medium I used for assignments: a webpage instead of a PowerPoint, or a game instead of a poster. To be honest, in these early attempts the computer science projects were more a carrot for engagement than a core component of the learning. Over time, however, I sought the intersection between the skills students needed to be successful in ELA and the skills they were developing through coding. As I created lessons and activities that integrated computational thinking and computer science concepts with the Common Core ELA standards, I found opportunities to make my instruction relevant to more students. After all, most of us likely interact with phones more than poetry.

Over the years, I gradually transitioned to a position as a full-time computer science teacher, and eventually a computer science curriculum developer and teacher facilitator, but I've never forgotten that moment when my students first made the connection between what they believed to be two disparate content areas.

The landscape has changed since I received a teaching endorsement. As of the writing of this book, computer science classes count toward graduation in 32 states and Washington D.C., 11 states have adopted computer science standards, and some are even offering endorsements to teach computer science. The field is growing, but there's still quite a ways to go, particularly given that computing jobs represent the number one source of new wages in the U.S., and half a million of those jobs are still unfilled due to a lack of graduates (Code.org, 2017a).

Integrating computer science into core academic classes serves two primary purposes. First, it provides an opportunity for students to experience computer science in schools where they otherwise wouldn't be afforded the opportunity. Second, it exposes students to the many contexts in which computer science can be applied in the real world.

Who Is This Book For?

You don't need any prior computer science or coding experience to use this book. My goal is to show you the natural overlaps between CS and core academic areas, with a specific focus on the needs of a middle-school class. In addition to the higher-level connections between computer science and each specific content area, I've selected a handful of classroom activities from the CS Unplugged website (www. csunplugged.org) that can be used to introduce computer science concepts without requiring any technology in the classroom. Finally, each content area section culminates in a coding project that has been tailored for that specific subject. These projects are designed for a variety of experience levels, from a very first experience with only a light amount of programming to a richer project that includes more computer science concepts.

Is It "Coding" or "Computer Science"?

Throughout this book I'll refer to both coding and computer science. While the two terms may seem interchangeable (and are often treated as such), the difference is important.

> **Coding** is the act of writing code for a computer to process.

> **Computer science** or **CS** is the study of the core principles of computing, including the processing of information, the design and interplay of hardware and software, and the applications of computing. Coding is frequently the way in which this study is conducted or expressed, but coding is merely one component of computer science.

For the Content Area Teacher

If you teach language arts, social studies, math, or science, this book is for you. In the appropriate content area section, you'll find support for bringing in core computer science concepts and practices (such as computational thinking) in a way that supports and strengthens your content area instruction. This support includes context about how the principles of computer science apply in your content area in the real world, as well as lesson and project ideas aligned to content area standards, designed to help your students make those connections in the classroom.

If you teach art, music, a foreign language, physical education, underwater basket-weaving, or any other content area, this book is also for you! While the structure is designed around the "core four," all of the ideas presented can be easily modified to fit the context of any number of classes. At the end of each project, you'll find some specific modification ideas for other contexts and content areas.

For the Technology or Computer Science Teacher

For those already teaching computer science or coding in some form, you'll find this book to be a useful foot in the door to build cross-curricular opportunities for your students. While all of these projects could be used without modification in your technology class, I urge you to use the content area contextual supports to work with your peers teaching other courses. Arguments for teaching computer science in each content area and the standards addressed are offered to help you make your case for initiating this collaboration.

By supporting your fellow teachers in their instruction, you'll get a chance to reach students who might not otherwise take your courses. This will also give you the chance to demonstrate the value of your course(s) to the school community at large, hopefully allowing you to build and strengthen your computer science program.

This Is Not a "How-to-Code" Book

There are lots of places to learn the basics of programming in any number of languages—that ground is well trod and supported elsewhere. The focus of this book is finding authentic opportunities for students to apply computer science skills in their core academic classes. While developing your own skills as a programmer is certainly an asset in this endeavor, it's not essential that you learn to code to apply the ideas and lessons in this book. You'll find the projects are quite approachable to new programmers. As long as you can embrace the lead-learner mindset (more on that in Chapter 1), you'll be just fine!

How To Use This Book

This book is broken into three primary sections.

> **Part I** introduces the core pedagogy, strategies, and tools that will be used throughout the rest of the book. Reading this section encourages you to consider the role computer science might play in your regular instruction, and what new instructional strategies you'll want to incorporate as you blaze a trail into becoming a teacher of computer science. The philosophy introduced in this section will help you transform your classroom and your instructional practice, while providing the context for how and why the later activities are designed in the way they are.

> **Part II** is organized into four subsections: language arts, social studies, science, and math. In each of these sections, I make the case for teaching computer science in that content area, with particular attention to the intersection between

each content area and the real-world applications of computer science, as well as any content-area specific considerations to keep in mind. From there, I explore offline activities from CS Unplugged that can be used as a computer-free introduction to the role computer science plays in each content area. Finally, each section culminates in a rich coding project designed to highlight ways in which computer science and each content area overlap in the real world, aligned to appropriate CSTA, ISTE, Common Core, and NGSS standards.

Part III deals with the more practical aspects of bringing computer science into the classroom. With the projects from Part II in mind, you can explore various approaches to assessment and student support. I offer a handful of approaches to assessing student work, including consideration of *what* you'll really want to assess when balancing your content-area standards and the computer science you've integrated. In addition, I'll broach the very real possibility that things won't always work for your students (astonishing!), and how to go about dealing with the inevitable bugs and issues that new programmers are sure to encounter.

Resources embedded in the book and featured in the Creative Coding Connection boxes found within each chapter offer ideas and tools for bringing computer science and coding to your students.

Appendixes are provided to help drive your growth as a computer science teacher. Specific resources are provided to get your classroom prepared for the necessary tools, and these include places to learn more about computer science and coding. I've also provided specific examples for how each coding project can be adapted to use different tools or programming languages, as appropriate.

Finally, you'll want to visit the companion website: **creativecodingbook.com**. That's where you'll find printable lesson resources, examples for each project, and lots of additional resources to help you on your journey of bringing computer science and coding into your classroom.

Let's dive in!

Tools and Strategies

This section looks at how computer science fits into regular instruction, and how to support and bring CS into daily lessons. The philosophy introduced in this section will help you transform your classroom and your instructional practice, while providing the context for activities in Part II. The chapters in this section explore:

- How coding and computer science can be incorporated into core content areas
- What computational thinking means
- How to teach coding and computational thinking across the curriculum

Teaching Computer Science in Core Content Areas

While building a computer science program at my own school, I constantly faced the question, why? Why should we make room for something else in an already packed schedule? Why can't kids just take AP computer science in high school? Why would kids even be interested in CS in the first place? I won't pretend that it's easy to implement changes in your school, and one of the benefits of infusing CS into existing classes is that you sidestep much of the bureaucracy that gets in the way of adding a whole new class, let alone an entirely new content area. That said, there are a lot of compelling arguments for bringing CS to the middle grades. Colleen Lewis, assistant professor of computer science at Harvey Mudd College, (2017) argues against some of the most common reasons for teaching computer science (e.g., proposing that computer science teaches logical-thinking skills) and instead proposes advocating for computer science education based on three main tenets:

1. **Computing is ubiquitous.** Universal, high-quality K–12 computer science instruction could provide all students the opportunities they need and deserve to understand the world around them. Early access to this lens on the world is essential for students to build a complete understanding of their world as they learn math, science, language arts, social studies, or any other subject.

2. **Cultural and structural barriers block students from pursuing computer science at the college level.** Universal, high-quality K–12 computer science instruction could serve as a protective factor for students. Introducing students to computer science before they have developed a sense of self ensures that computer science may be a part of that sense of self.

3. **Computer science jobs are high paying and high status.** Universal, high-quality K–12 computer science instruction could increase access to the growing number of high-paying, high-status jobs in computer science and related fields. This universal access is an essential step in dismantling the existing systemic barriers in the industry that prevent equitable participation, particularly by women and people of color. (Lewis, 2017)

As an administrator or policy maker, these arguments are both powerful and fairly unassailable. From the perspective of an on-the-ground teacher, however, they lack the practicality required for the administration's support. In that light, and with the goal of integrating computer science into existing courses in mind, I've compiled my top five arguments for computer science integration in middle school.

1. It's a Foundational Skill

President Obama declared that coding is no longer an optional skill; it's a basic skill. We teach students about the digestive and circulatory systems not because we expect all students to become doctors, but because we expect engaged citizens to have a fundamental understanding of the world. I would argue that how the internet or a smartphone works is *at least* as essential as the basic biology that we teach all students. How do we expect students to engage thoughtfully in discussions around internet regulation, information privacy, or the role of artificial intelligence without a baseline understanding of computer science?

2. It's an Empowering Tool for Self-Expression

Setting aside the essential role that technology plays in society, there's a perfectly reasonable argument for teaching computer science: it's fun! More than that, programming is a powerful medium for personal expression unlike anything that has come before it. For students who find solace and expression in art, music, performance, writing, or any other expressive outlet you can imagine, coding can boost their expressive potential.

3. It's an Integral Part of the Standards

The Next Generation Science Standards (NGSS) explicitly calls out both computational thinking and computer modeling as essential elements of a K–12 science education, though few packaged science curricula incorporate the computer science and programming necessary to support these standards (National Research Council, 2013). If we value science education, computer science is an essential component. While the Common Core math standards don't feature the same explicit language, they do share deep commonalities with the K–12 Computer Science Framework, particularly the eight math practices (National Governors Association Center for Best Practices, & Council of Chief State School Officers, 2018). Taking advantage of these overlapping practices will give students the opportunity to see math as more authentic and applicable as they use it to compose programs that they care about. Additionally, the ISTE Standards for Students, which are designed to guide instruction using technology across all content areas, explicitly call out computational thinking while containing deep connections to other areas of computer science (2016).

4. It's Core to Digital Citizenship

I have yet to find a school administrator who doesn't appreciate the need for our students to develop digital citizenship skills, but how many truly appreciate what that means? A fundamental understanding of the internet's systems and the data they collect is essential for students to understand their responsibilities as citizens. We teach civics because we expect students to be active citizens in our society. Civic engagement requires an understanding of the foundational structures upon which our society is built, as well as the systems of governance that keep it running. How can we expect students to become digital citizens if they have no understanding of the foundational structures of the internet or its systems of governance? How many of our students have any understanding of who controls access to their digital society? Who makes the rules? How can we, as citizens, be active participants in this digital society?

5. It's a Civil Rights Issue

I would say that a basic understanding of computer science is essential to being an active member of society in the future, but that future is already here. Whether it's net neutrality, cryptocurrencies, credit card security breaches, the safety of self-driving cars, the security implications of home automation, or any number of other issues, it's becoming clearer every day that society is facing problems that most of us are ill-equipped to understand, which makes making informed decisions impossible. Those members of the next generation who don't learn about computer science will be left at the mercy of those who do. Students without a basic computer science education will be excluded from jobs (a civil rights issue of its own), and the ability to understand the technological components of society will define the "haves" and the "have-nots" of the future.

Teaching computer science to our students is more than a great idea; it's a fundamental responsibility that our schools can no longer ignore. If we don't give students access to this knowledge, we're effectively preventing them from becoming active and empowered citizens of both our digital and physical societies, as the two become ever more entwined.

Can I Teach Computer Science without a CS Background?

You're probably teaching your specific subject area because you have been deemed "highly qualified" to teach it. Maybe your undergraduate degree was in English, or you came to Science teaching after a career as a biologist. More likely than not, you are some manner of subject matter expert in addition to being a master of the art of teaching. So, what qualifies you to teach computer science? You may not have the expertise to which you're accustomed, but you *can* leverage your status as a novice to model for your students what lifelong learning and growth looks like. It's not always easy to learn alongside your students, but it's the perfect opportunity to practice what we preach.

People who work in computer science related fields are rarely experts, and programmers are always learning, always trying to keep up with their rapidly changing field. As a new-to-CS teacher, you too will always be learning and keeping up with the changes. While a teacher with more content knowledge may start in a different place, the truth is that *all* computer science teachers are constantly learning and redeveloping their skill sets. Welcome to the team!

If you are still unconvinced, stick with me. In the next chapter, I'll offer some specific strategies to help, and you can always check the appendix for external resources to develop and hone your skills. The most important thing to remember is that you don't need to be, nor should you be, the source of all knowledge in your class.

The *All* in *Computer Science for All*

It's no secret that the representation of women and people of color has been dismal in the technology industry. According to a Gallup poll conducted by Google in 2016, students of color are significantly less likely to have access to dedicated computer science courses at school, or to even have access to a computer at home. Girls are not only less likely to learn computer science, but they're less likely to even be aware of the CS learning opportunities available to them. The systemic issues that prevent underrepresented populations from entering the field, and subsequently drive many of them out once they make it through the door, must be addressed much earlier. We'll never reach a place in which everyone has equal access to the world of technology unless we break down barriers and stereotypes much earlier (Google Inc. & Gallup Inc., 2016).

Middle school is an essential moment in the development of self-image because students transition to a school environment where their interests play a larger role in the development of a social cohort. This makes the middle-school years a crucial time to ensure that technical ability is a part of that self-image. Embedding computer science into required core academic courses is a great step in ensuring that all of our students get the opportunity to try this stuff out early, but availability alone is not enough. To truly address the issues in the field of technology, we need to do more than merely ensure all students have *equal* opportunities; we need to give them *equitable* opportunities.

Equity versus Equality

While I take issue with the popular graphic portraying the difference between equity and equality (Shouldn't we be tearing down the fence?), I do appreciate its ability to clarify the difference between the two (see Figure 1.1). Providing equity means that students receive what they *need* for success. Many of our students come through the door needing more—whether it's because they have stereotypes to overcome, lack access to the tools that other students have, or have learning challenges that require more or different support. To acknowledge this is to also acknowledge that some students will receive less, because they need less. We have to be realistic about our time and ability to support students, and prioritizing those who need it most can be a difficult choice to make. It's tempting to invest our energy in the advanced student who is engaged and outwardly appreciative of our time, but that's not the student for whom we can make the greatest impact.

For many underrepresented populations, stereotypes about who can become a programmer are the first barrier to break down.

When you bring computer science into your classroom, consider *who* it is you're engaging, and *how*. Here's a quick checklist that can help you identify places where you may be losing those underrepresented students, along with approaches to make them feel welcome and capable.

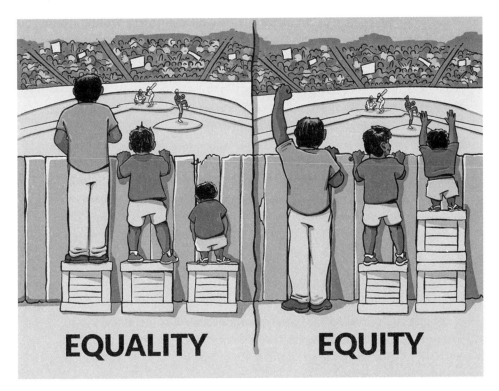

Figure 1.1: Equity and Equality. Source: Interaction Institute for Social Change | Artist: Angus Maguire

HOW MIGHT YOUR CLASSROOM ENVIRONMENT REINFORCE STEREOTYPES?

I've self-identified as a geek for having a personal identity, and in a classroom designed solely to express my own personal interests I might decorate with trinkets that celebrate that identity. Maybe I'd throw up a sweet Star Wars poster, or a model of the U.S.S. Enterprise. I might even tell myself that decorating in this way creates an environment that feels more welcoming for other students who, like myself as a child, feel like outsiders because of their interests. How, though, might those choices I make in decorating a classroom that reflects my own personality reinforce stereotypes about who does computer science? The environment that you create in your classroom has a strong impact on how your students develop sense of belonging, and the objects you decorate with send "ambient identity cues" that can actually impact students' interest and engagement with computer science. This doesn't mean that your walls need to be bare, or that you can't embed your personality into your classroom, but be thoughtful about the messages you might inadvertently send. Consider decorating based on a classroom interest survey, so you can incorporate things that make all students feel welcome.

IS THE CODING VERSION OF A PROJECT OPTIONAL?

If students have to opt in to coding before believing they are capable, they'll likely never do it. Make sure that, at least the first time around, the coding project is mandatory for everyone. There's nothing wrong with allowing students to opt in or out of using code as their medium of choice all of the time, but they need to be comfortable making that choice before we can expect them to dive in. It is similar to introducing a new food to a picky toddler—students may need multiple experiences with this new world to find the confidence that they like it and can do it. Create multiple opportunities for students to develop their skills and confidence as a whole team.

ARE YOUR EXPERIENCED STUDENTS DRIVING THE DIRECTION OF THE CLASS?

It's natural to rely on your experienced students to support yourself and the rest of the class, but consider what that communicates to students who come to you without background knowledge. If you want your experienced students to give support, provide them the structure to do so in a way that doesn't step on toes or intimidate others.

ARE THE SAME SKILLSETS ALWAYS IN THE SPOTLIGHT?

Consider ways that your students might feel less capable than their peers based on what skillsets seem valued in your class. Computer science is a large and varied field; there are many important roles to develop and roles to play. Make sure you find ways to celebrate the contributions of all students, and to find opportunities for every student to take the lead.

Integrating Computer Science Projects and Activities

The primary focus of this book is to support teachers in integrating computer science, computational thinking, and coding into other content areas. To do so, it's useful to consider approaches to integrating a new technology in general. When incorporating a new technology into the classroom, we run the risk of "teaching a tool" rather than using the tool to support learning objectives. You could, for example, spend a month walking students through the mechanics of replicating a specific app in App Lab. Students might successfully replicate the app, and they might even have fun doing it, but they may never learn: (a) how to build something of their own; or (b) *any* domain-specific content. So, before we dig into *how* we

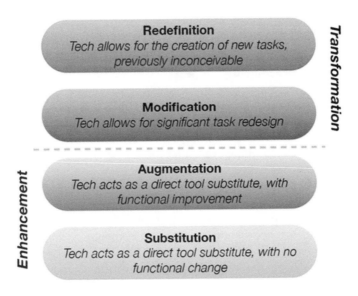

Figure 1.2: Substitution, Augmentation, Modification, and Redefinition (SAMR).

might integrate coding into a domain-specific project, let's first consider *what* we want students to get out of it.

The SAMR model for technology integration, popularized by Dr. Ruben Puentedura, is a great starting point for how we might approach integrating computer science into another content area (Puentedura, 2014). This model consists of four levels of integrating a technology into the classroom, each increasing in richness, from substitution, to augmentation, modification, and finally, redefinition (see Figure 1.2). The idea behind SAMR is that we can increase the richness and power of technology integration as we move through the stages. A new technology used purely as substitution for an analog medium might be more fun or engaging for some students, but it fails to take advantage of new learning experiences that a given technology can unlock.

I like this framework for thinking critically about how and why we invest energy into integrating new technologies into our classrooms, and as a tool to help teachers evaluate where they can improve the richness of their technology integration. The trouble with applying the SAMR model to computer science integration is that it assumes, by design, that the technology being integrated brings with it no additional learning objects. This is fine when you're looking to integrate a tool and want to avoid "teaching the tool," but that's not the case when we bring CS into the

Table 1.1 **The SEAA Model for Computer Science Integration**

STAGE	DESCRIPTION
Substitution	Computer science is used as a drop-in replacement for another medium. The computer science concepts aren't essential to the activity, and the created product is effectively similar to one completed without computer science.
Enrichment	Computer science is used to enrich an activity in ways that are impossible without it. The computer science concepts taught here are present as a means to an end; they enable a type of creation that enriches the content-area learning.
Authentic Application	Computer science is applied in a way that mirrors the real-world authentic applications within a given content area. In this stage the compter-science content and the subject area content are of equal importance, because they are married in a way that reflects use in the real world.

classroom. When it comes to integrating computer science, I'm still interested in how it can be used as a tool to teach other content, but I *also* want to teach students about the field of computer science and the specific skills associated with it. For this reason, I propose a new framework, inspired by SAMR but modified to take into account the balance we want to strike between teaching the core academic content and new computer science content. Let's call this the SEAA (Substitution, Enrichment, and Authentic Application) model (see Table 1.1).

Let's use a stand-in activity to consider how this model might be applied. This project is, before integration, a poster project about a local proposed zoning change in a social studies class. Students research the three different zoning proposals, then create a poster that highlights the pros and cons of each proposal.

When considering my proposed model, the substitution stage is essentially the same. Activities at this level fail to effectively harness the power of computing, and they do little to bring computer science to more students. At this stage, our poster might just be replaced with a Scratch project. Students might add some animations, sounds, or interactions, but there's nothing essential at this stage that couldn't also be effectively communicated through the original medium.

The enrichment stage covers augmentation and a portion of modification. Activities enriched with computer science enable students to create artifacts that would be otherwise impossible or unfeasible. At this stage, our original Scratch project might ask viewers to pick which zoning change they prefer, tracking the popularity of each choice with a variable. This would allow students to see how people responded to their presented information in a way that would be difficult without computer science.

The authentic application stage is the focus of the lessons in this book, and the most powerful form of computer science integration. At this stage, a blend of the modification and redefinition stages of SAMR, computer science, and the primary content area are entwined based on how people work in the "real" world. At this stage, our zoning change project could take a number of different turns. One approach would be to build a simple model of the impacts of each change, allowing users to interact with the changes in a more hands-on fashion. Alternatively, you could build on the data tracking from the enrichment example, but instead track people's preconceptions before and after interacting with the presentation to understand how the presentation changed perceptions, or gather multiple points of data to identify which elements of each zoning change people responded to and develop a fourth proposal to address those reposes. In either case, we're taking the project from an isolated in-classroom activity, and integrating computer science in the same way a city planner would to make the project more real.

Computer Science Practices

In 2016 a coalition of organizations—including the Association for Computing Machinery, Code.org, the Computer Science Teachers Association, the Cyber Innovation Center, and the National Math and Science Initiative, and computer science educators in both K–12 and higher education—set out to establish a framework that identified the foundational concepts and practices that should be taught in kindergarten through 12th grade (see the framework at **k12cs.org**) The resulting K–12 Computer Science Framework has become the basis for many standards efforts across the U.S., including the 2017 revision of the Computer Science Teachers Association (CSTA) standards (**csteachers.org/page/standards**). This framework can serve as a useful tool in developing computer science integration, as it establishes the concepts and practices appropriate to teach at each grade level and which are applicable across a number of different standards frameworks that may vary across states.

While the projects in this book contain many of the computer science concepts in the framework, please focus on the practices as the primary tools for planning integration (see Table 1.2). By pairing these practices with content-area specific standards, we ensure that what students are *doing* (computer science) supports what they should *know* (your subject-area content).

Table 1.2   K–12 Computer Science Framework Practices

PRACTICE	DESCRIPTION
1. **Fostering an Inclusive Computing Culture**	Building an inclusive and diverse computing culture requires strategies for incorporating perspectives from people of different genders, ethnicities, and abilities. Incorporating these perspectives involves understanding the personal, ethical, social, economic, and cultural contexts in which people operate. Considering the needs of diverse users during the design process is essential to producing inclusive computational products.
2. **Collaborating around Computing**	Collaborative computing is the process of performing a computational task by working in pairs and on teams. Because it involves asking for the contributions and feedback of others, effective collaboration can lead to better outcomes than working independently. Collaboration requires individuals to navigate and incorporate diverse perspectives, conflicting ideas, disparate skills, and distinct personalities. Students should use collaborative tools to effectively work together and to create complex artifacts.
3. **Recognizing and Defining Computational Problems**	The ability to recognize appropriate and worthwhile opportunities to apply computation is a skill that develops over time and is central to computing. Solving a problem with a computational approach requires defining the problem, breaking it down into parts, and evaluating each part to determine whether a computational solution is appropriate.

Table 1.2 K–12 Computer Science Framework Practices

PRACTICE	DESCRIPTION
4. **Developing and Using Abstractions**	Abstractions are formed by identifying patterns and extracting common features from specific examples to create generalizations. Using generalized solutions and parts of solutions designed for broad reuse simplifies the development process by managing complexity.
5. **Creating Computational Artifacts**	The process of developing computational artifacts embraces both creative expression and the exploration of ideas to create prototypes and solve computational problems. Students create artifacts that are personally relevant or beneficial to their community and beyond. Computational artifacts can be created by combining and modifying existing artifacts or by developing new artifacts. Examples of computational artifacts include programs, simulations, visualizations, digital animations, robotic systems, and apps.
6. **Testing and Refining Computational Artifact**	Testing and refinement is the deliberate and iterative process of improving a computational artifact. This process includes debugging (identifying and fixing errors) and comparing actual outcomes to intended outcomes. Students also respond to the changing needs and expectations of end users and improve the performance, reliability, usability, and accessibility of artifacts.
7. **Communicating about Computing**	Communication involves personal expression and exchanging ideas with others. In computer science, students communicate with diverse audiences about the use and effects of computation and the appropriateness of computational choices. Students write clear comments, document their work, and communicate their ideas through multiple forms of media. Clear communication includes using precise language and carefully considering possible audiences.

CORE PRACTICES
INCLUDING COMPUTATIONAL THINKING

Figure 1.3: K-12 Computer Science Framework Core Practices.

Computational Thinking

The concept of computational thinking has been around for quite a while, most recently repopularized by Jeannette Wing in a 2006 article for the Association for Computing Machinery. Despite its popularity as a catch phrase, people have differing (and even competing) definitions for computational thinking. In 2011 the CSTA and ISTE worked to define computational thinking and how it can be used in the classroom, with the *Computational Thinking Leadership Toolkit*. As part of this toolkit, the CSTA and ISTE codeveloped the following operational definition for computational thinking that can help ground our common understanding.

Computational thinking is a problem-solving process that includes (but is not limited to) the following characteristics:

- formulating problems in a way that enables us to use a computer and other tools to help solve them;

- logically organizing and analyzing data;

- representing data through abstractions, such as models and simulations;

- identifying, analyzing, and implementing possible solutions with the goal of achieving the most efficient and effective combination of steps and resources; and

- generalizing and transferring this problem-solving process to a wide variety of problems.

These skills are supported and enhanced by a number of dispositions or attitudes that are essential dimensions of computational thinking. These dispositions or attitudes include:

- confidence in dealing with complexity;

- persistence in working with difficult problems;

- tolerance for ambiguity;

- the ability to deal with open ended problems; and

- the ability to communicate and work with others to achieve a common goal or solution (p. 13).

If you compare this with the previous seven practices of the K-12 Computer Science Framework, you should notice a great deal of overlap. The framework's authors embedded computational thinking within the practices to ensure that they were a grounding element of the framework, without being limited to considering only computational thinking. In particular, practices 3-6 (Recognizing and

Defining Computational Problems, Developing and Using Abstractions, Creating Computational Artifacts, and Testing and Refining Computational Artifacts), reflect the core elements of computational thinking, while practices 1, 2, and 7 incorporate more general-purpose practices that complement computer science. For the sake of clarity, I focus on specific framework practices, with the understanding that computational thinking is embedded.

Connecting to the ISTE Standards for Students

If you're at all familiar with the ISTE Standards for Students, you may have noticed many similarities in reading through the K–12 Computer Science Framework Practices. Both of these documents paint a picture of students well prepared to engage and thrive in a rapidly changing world. The two are so close in scope and vision that you can find each of the seven practices embedded within the ISTE Standards

Table 1.3 Connecting the ISTE Standards for Students and the K–12 Computer Science Framework Practices

ISTE STANDARDS FOR STUDENTS	K–12 COMPUTER SCIENCE FRAMEWORK PRACTICE
Empowered Learner	Testing and Refining Computational Artifacts
Digital Citizen	Fostering an Inclusive Computing Culture
Knowledge Constructor	Recognizing and Defining Computational Problems
Innovative Designer	Creating Computational Artifacts Testing and Refining Computational Artifacts
Computational Thinker	Recognizing and Defining Computational Problems Developing and Using Abstractions Creating Computational Artifacts Testing and Refining Computational Artifacts
Creative Communicator	Communicating About Computing
Global Collaborator	Fostering an Inclusive Computing Culture Collaborating Around Computing

for Students (see Table 1.3). The full text of the ISTE Standards for Students appears in Appendix D.

Taking Your First (or Next) Step

I've been out of the classroom for a few years now, but my teaching muscles are not so atrophied that I don't suffer a twinge when thinking about adding something new to a class. I have no doubt that every teacher reading this could come up with a laundry list of the things you've been "volun-told" to find room for in your schedule. Add the overflowing bucket of standards you're expected to address, whichever district initiatives are hot this season, and so on and so forth. Who in their right mind could expect you to find room for something new?

I can't take anything off your plate, and I can't decrease the load of learning objectives your students are already expected to meet. I *can* promise you that the activities and projects in this book are designed to support your instruction of content-area standards, and I believe you can find room in your course where these lessons can replace existing ones. Integrating computer science will enable you to engage students in new ways, infuse more fun into your classroom, and break through to some of your harder-to-reach students. It will bring new life to your existing curriculum by highlighting the natural connections among computer science, technology, and your content-area standards. I can't promise you that this won't take work, but I ask you to trust that it will be *worthwhile* work.

I also want to acknowledge that we can't do everything at once. The best thing you can do for your students is to always be taking the next step forward. As you move through this book and begin considering the implications of these ideas and activities in your classroom, I'd like you to keep in mind the SEA model for computer science integration I've proposed. This tool is not intended to set a gold standard for what you *should* be doing, but to help you see places where you *could* do more. Your students will not always be working at the Authentic Application end of the spectrum, and that's fine—even desirable. It's a lot of work to build truly authentic integrated experiences, and sometimes it's enough to just have fun with code in place of having fun with posters and markers. If, by the end of this book, you feel like you're just going to supplement a lesson with some code, that's fantastic! Take the first step.

Classroom Strategies

Introducing coding into the classroom can be an intimidating prospect for a teacher without any computer science experience. What happens when students have issues you don't understand? What about that one kid who knows far more than you do? How can you answer all of your students' questions if you've never done this before?

Take a breath.

As you bring this exciting, new content into your classroom, give yourself permission to take small steps. Give yourself permission to struggle, flail, and even fail. In addition to that advice, I've got some useful strategies for you to keep in your back pocket. Some of these may be familiar to you, as they are built on widely recognized good practices for student-centered learning. Some have been adapted from best practices in the technology industry, which make may them seem uniquely suited to teaching computer science. This doesn't make then unsuitable to application in other content areas. For those, consider how they may be applied more broadly in conjunction with your existing teaching practices.

Become the Lead Learner

We ask a lot of our students. We ask them to live in a rigidly structured environment and follow rules they don't always understand; more than anything, we ask them to constantly learn. This may seem obvious, but consider what we're really asking of students: to constantly, all day, try to do things that they've never done before (or never done well). We consistently ask them to take risks in an environment where the consequences of failure seem dire.

It would behoove educators to empathize with that student experience a bit more, to place ourselves in a situation that requires us to constantly take risks and try new things. Being a lead learner means giving up your role as the fount of knowledge in the classroom and embracing your role as a fellow knowledge seeker. Certainly, there are always times for you to share your experience with your students, but as the lead learner in the classroom you'll also need to become comfortable saying, "I don't know, let's find out." As you and your students embark on this journey together, be honest with your students about your own strengths and weaknesses. Model for them what it looks like to embrace challenges and learn.

Embracing your role as lead learner in a way that is transparent to your students, you can turn a lack of experience with computer science into a benefit. The Code. org Computer Science Discoveries course (2017c) recommends a handful of actionable ways to teach as a lead learner:

Lead learner Strategies

- Allow students to dive into an activity without presenting all the content first.

- Encourage students to rely on each other for support.

- Don't give the answer right away, even if you know it.

- Feel open to making mistakes in front of students so that they see it is part of the learning process.

- Ask students questions that direct their attention toward the issue to investigate without giving away what they need to change.

- Model the steps you would go through as a learner of a new subject. Explain the different questions you ask yourself along the way and the ways you go about finding answers (p. 5).

You'll note that the goal in all of these approaches is not to abdicate yourself of having or acquiring content knowledge, but rather to make visible to your students the process through which you acquire new knowledge. By truly embracing the role of a lead learner, you will naturally develop deeper content knowledge and become a better computer science teacher. The beauty of this field is that it is constantly evolving. No one knows all the answers. Programmers are constantly learning, always reinventing their skill sets. Isn't that the mindset we want for our students—to constantly be growing and learning? Computer science requires participants to be lifelong learners.

The lead-learner approach is rooted in Carol Dweck's (2006) research of the growth mindset. The concept of a growth mindset, as opposed to a fixed mindset, is based in the neuroscience of brain plasticity—the idea that our brains are capable of change and growth. A student (or teacher) with a fixed mindset may believe that

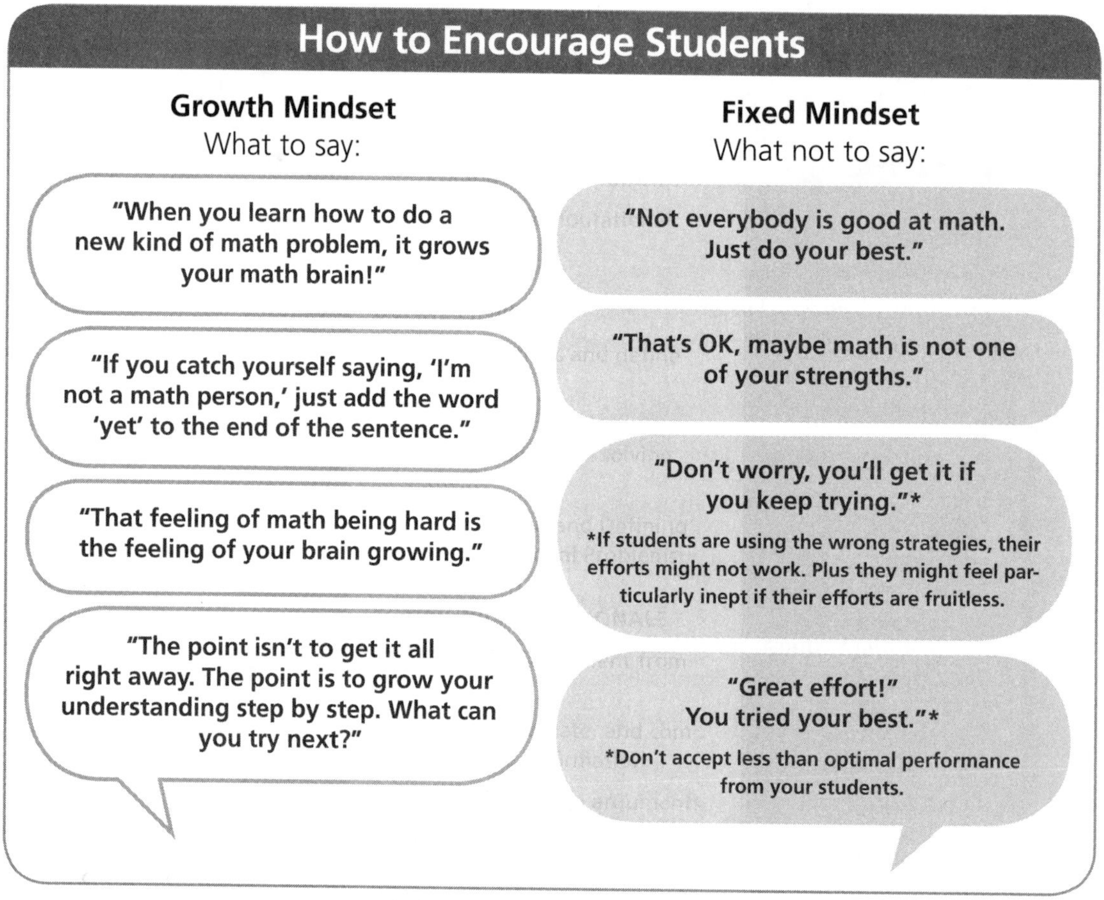

How to Encourage Students

Growth Mindset
What to say:

"When you learn how to do a new kind of math problem, it grows your math brain!"

"If you catch yourself saying, 'I'm not a math person,' just add the word 'yet' to the end of the sentence."

"That feeling of math being hard is the feeling of your brain growing."

"The point isn't to get it all right away. The point is to grow your understanding step by step. What can you try next?"

Fixed Mindset
What not to say:

"Not everybody is good at math. Just do your best."

"That's OK, maybe math is not one of your strengths."

"Don't worry, you'll get it if you keep trying."*

*If students are using the wrong strategies, their efforts might not work. Plus they might feel particularly inept if their efforts are fruitless.

"Great effort!" You tried your best."*

*Don't accept less than optimal performance from your students.

Figure 2.1: Encouraging a Growth Mindset. Source: Carol Dweck

they are naturally predisposed to be good at some things and bad at other things, and that there is no overcoming such predisposition. In computer science, this fixed mindset is reinforced by the mythical (and debunked) "geek gene"– the thing that determines whether you've got it, or you don't (Patitsas et al., 2016). By actively encouraging your students to adopt a growth mindset, you can help them overcome the internal or cultural barriers that lead many to believe that they "can't do" computer science. I can't hope to do full justice to the growth mindset concept here, and I highly encourage you to read Dweck's book to get a deeper understanding, but I do have recommendations for simple changes in the way you talk to your students that will help you to reinforce a growth mindset (see Figure 2.1).

Table 2.1 **Lead Learner Phrasebook** *[handwritten: When they know more than you do]*

STUDENT STATEMENT	LEAD-LEARNER RESPONSE
"What can we make with this tool?"	Point them toward a gallery of existing works in that language to try and find examples.
"My code doesn't work, can you fix it?"	Avoid the temptation to try and fix problems, but ask the student to talk through what their code should do and provide them with debugging strategies from Chapter 9.
"I'm trying to do _____, can you help me figure it out?"	Ask them to teach you about the techniques with which you are unfamiliar. Often, just explaining your code to someone else will reveal the issues.
"Why aren't we programming in _____ instead of _____. This is for kids."	Let the student know that every language has its pros and cons, and that you chose this one for the reasons laid out in the previous chapter. If they persist, encourage the student to replicate the class projects in their preferred language and share with you how it compared to your chosen language.
"This isn't how it really works, why don't you know how it really works?"	Often in computer science we simplify concepts when they are first introduced, filling in the details later. Let the student know this, and ask if they'd like to come up with a way to fill in the details and teach it to the class.

What to Do When You Don't Know

It's still helpful to have some specific techniques in your back pocket to rely on when those lead-learner moments come up. I've compiled a handful of phrases to help with common lead-learner experiences in Table 2.1.

Communication and Collaboration

Another essential skill for programmers is the ability to communicate and collaborate with others—often remotely, and often across cultures and languages. This is a skill that we generally value for all students, but it comes into clearer focus when approached through the lens of computer science. The projects I've presented are designed for collaboration, but an effective collaborative classroom doesn't happen without thoughtful work from the teacher.

If your classroom is anything like a typical American classroom, you're already supporting a wide range of abilities when it comes to your content area, and I'm sure you've developed and adopted strategies to address the need for differentiation across skill levels. You are very likely to have an even wider range of skill sets in your classroom when it comes to programming. Because computer science is not (yet) a core part of most students' school experience, you will almost certainly encounter students who have absolutely no experience with it. Some students, on the other hand, will come in having learned a bit in grade school, in a club, or even independently at home. Many more will arrive eager yet inexperienced. Your challenge is to balance all of those students, ensuring that each feels welcome and capable. The way in which you choose to manage these varied experience levels can have a significant impact on the self-efficacy and self-perception of traditionally underrepresented students (Barker, McDowell, & Kalahar, 2009).

Pair Programming

Pair programming is a technique borrowed from the software-development industry, in which two programmers work side-by-side on the same computer to solve a problem. While the idea of two people doing the work of one seems wasteful, well-executed pair programming has been proven to improve the quality of code as well as the quality of team communication. One study found a number of specific benefits that software developers saw after implementing pair programming (Cockburn & Williams, 2000, p. 9), including:

- Many mistakes get caught as they are being typed in rather than in QA test or in the field.

- The end defect content is statistically lower.

- The designs are better and the code length is shorter.

- The team solves problems faster.

- The programmers learn significantly more, about the system and about software development.

- The project ends up with multiple people understanding each piece of the system.

- The programmers learn to work together and talk more often together, giving better information flow and team dynamics.

- Programmers enjoy their work more.

These benefits are great for a company that wants to make a better product, but they're even better for students who want to develop their programming skills.. Pair programming has been effectively implemented in K–12 and beyond as a tool to improve computer science learning while at the same time improving products that students create and classes' communication and collaboration (Williams & Upchurch, 2001; McDowell et al., 2003; McDowell et al., 2006). Moreover, pair programming has been shown to decrease the gender gap by demonstrating that programming is a collaborative and social activity, instead of a competitive and isolated one (Werner, Hanks, & McDowell, 2004).

When using pair programming in the classroom, student pairs will take on two roles. The **driver** is responsible for actually controlling the mouse and keyboard and creating the code. The **navigator** works with the driver to ensure that what they are creating meets the goal they set out to achieve. The navigator reads the code that the driver writes, asks questions, and makes suggestions about what to do next. The two switch roles frequently (every 3–5 minutes) to ensure that both students contribute equally and remain engaged in the activity. In industry, this strategy has proven to create more reliable, and often more creative code than that created by individuals working alone. When implementing pair programming, keep the following ground rules in mind.

PAIR-PROGRAMMING GUIDELINES

1. Only the driver may touch the mouse and keyboard. No backseat driving!

2. Switch up roles frequently (every 3–5 minutes).

3. Talk! Driver and navigator should be constantly communicating about what they're making.

4. Read! The navigator should be able to explain all of the code that the driver is writing.

Structures for Peer Support and Instruction

Relying on your skilled or experienced students to support your inexperienced ones can be a powerful tool in building a supportive and collaborative classroom community, if managed effectively. It can also be demoralizing and damaging to student self-efficacy if you don't establish clear guidelines. Let's explore a quick scenario to see how peer support might play out both positively and negatively.

Gabriel is a student who has never coded before. Gabriel doesn't have a computer at home, and when he's been required to use computers at school, he's never really felt successful or comfortable. Gabriel's social studies teacher has announced that for their next project the class will be making apps to address a need of a pioneer in the early 1800s. Gabriel is struggling with the assignment and is having a hard time understanding how to make a button click change screens. The teacher asks Sam, a student who has been going to coding clubs for years and has already finished her project, to help Gabriel.

SCENARIO A

Sam sits down next to Gabriel, takes the mouse, and shows how to drag out the blocks needed to make the button change screens. Sam asks if Gabriel understands how it works, and then runs off to help someone else.

SCENARIO B

Sam sits down next to Gabriel and asks what they want the program to do. Gabriel explains that it should change screens when the button is clicked, and Sam asks Gabriel to look through the toolbox to see if there's a block that looks like it might respond to a click. Together they talk through what the different blocks might do until Gabriel finds one that seems like it might work. Sam encourages Gabriel to try it out, and watches to see if it worked. Before leaving, Sam asks Gabriel to explain what they programmed to make sure Gabriel fully understands. When another student comes up against the same problem, Sam asks Gabriel to go over and help.

In each of those scenarios, how do you think Gabriel was left feeling about his programming abilities at the end of the encounter? In scenario A, Gabriel didn't actually *do* any of the programming, and while the problem was solved, it's unclear whether Gabriel actually learned anything. Meanwhile, Sam is allowed to feel (and be viewed by others in the class) like a hero, hopping from computer to computer, solving problems all the way. Is Sam just naturally better at computers? Should Gabriel even try, knowing that Sam (and maybe everyone else) is so much better at this?

While scenario B is a much more involved process, it seems far more likely that Gabriel learned how to use the command to respond to a click. Sam doesn't get the immediate gratification of looking like a hero, but does get the satisfaction of actually *teaching* someone else. In the process, Sam is modeling to Gabriel her own problem-solving process in a way that demystifies Sam's programming aptitude and makes it seem more approachable. By the end, Gabriel has not only learned the content, but has also been placed in the role of peer support for others, showing that everyone is able to master this.

Clearly, scenario B is the kind of scene we'd like to see in our classrooms. Even acknowledging that everything won't always go so smoothly, that the Gabriels in your class won't always "get it" so quickly, or that the Sams won't always have the patience to let the Gabriels do the hard work, it's still a step toward a healthier classroom community, in which students of all experience levels can feel success-ful. To reach this kind of classroom, we have to do more than ask our high fliers to "help." We need to build and reinforce structures for *all* students to feel like successful computer science students and important contributors to the classroom community. Here are a few guidelines to help develop the kind of collaborative peer support that we're looking for.

ASK THREE BEFORE ME
To ensure that students have an opportunity to provide support to each other without your intervention, force them to seek help from the class before reaching out to you. It is very straightforward: a student must ask three other students for support before asking the teacher.

ASSIGN ROLES
Students need to have clear and consistent roles when serving in a peer-support scenario. I like to rely on the roles that we've already developed to support pair programming: **driver** and **navigator**. Students offering peer support should always be in the **navigator** role, meaning no touching of the mouse or keyboard, and no dictating what the driver should do—just providing guidance.

SET BOUNDARIES
Sometimes we want to struggle through a problem without someone else's input. Establish tools for students to set their own boundaries for getting support. I like to use nonverbal tools that let students express their needs for support while still working. Traffic light cups work great for this. All students get a green, yellow, and red SOLO cup to stack on their desk. Whichever cup is on the top

of the stack communicates their need for assistance. Green = everything is fine, yellow = struggling, but not yet in need of assistance, and red = blocked and in need of help.

FIND OPPORTUNITIES FOR **ALL** STUDENTS TO GIVE AND RECEIVE SUPPORT
In scenario B, both Sam and Gabriel got chances to support their peers. This opportunity is a powerful tool to build or repair student self-efficacy, so it's well worth seeking out places for every student to experience it. Not all students may be in a position to provide peer support with programming, but there are many other places where you can highlight the wide range of skill-sets and abilities present in your classroom. Consider identifying students that can help their peers with text copy, graphics, interface design, or idea generation.

Authenticity and Ownership

Programming sometimes gets a bad rap for being boring, uncreative, and isolating. None of that's actually true, but sometimes perception dictates reality. Break that stereotype by showing students authentic uses for computer science and giving them ownership over how they engage with those authentic applications. Take, for example, a student who cares deeply about environmental conservation and hasn't seen programming as anything more than a tool for making games that they don't care about. For that student, learning about how computer scientists are using computational sustainability to better understand the connections between changing weather and bird migrations might be the connection they need to see CS in a new, more authentically valuable, light (Gomes, 2009). Computer science is, quite literally, everywhere. Making explicit the role of computer science in specific fields that a student cares about helps them to envision how learning CS might empower them to create real and meaningful change.

Student Choice

Giving students choices is one of those things that *feels* simple but actually requires more of educators to ensure that the choices are authentic. To choose between creating a poster and a PowerPoint is relatively meaningless if the student cannot choose the assignment's topic. Instead, consider constraining their options of how to complete a project (e.g., what tools they use or skills they apply), but allow students to personally invest in the topic of their inquiry.

The challenge, of course, is to ensure that students can meet the educational outcomes that we want to see, regardless of the topic they choose to pursue. In computer science this might mean requiring students to use a given set of skills (e.g., functions or *for* loops) but allowing them to choose the way in which they demonstrate mastery of those skills.

Social Impact

Few advancements have had the scale of social impact that the advent of ubiquitous computing has had. Technology has fundamentally changed the way the world works, connected people in new ways, and enabled citizens to engage with the world in powerful ways. The so-called "sharing economy," exemplified by apps such as Uber and Airbnb, has created new ways for people to share and profit off of their resources, while raising lots of questions about the traditional relationship between employer and employee, government regulation, and the evolution of our social contracts (Heinrichs, 2013). Cryptocurrencies such as Bitcoin allow for people to make financial transactions that circumvent the traditional economy (Vigna & Casey, 2016). Embedding social relevance in your instruction can open your students' eyes to the power and ethical implications of computing, engaging many students who might otherwise think that computing is merely frivolous (Buckley, Nordlinger, & Subramanian, 2008).

"Apps for Good" *curriculum*

The Apps for Good curriculum and competition out of the United Kingdom has been empowering students to create powerful and impactful apps since 2010 (Visit their website at www.appsforgood.org.). The range of student-created apps that have come out of the program reflect our students' passion and care for their society. Given the chance to effect change through technology, students have developed apps to support people dealing with grief, help the elderly contact emergency assistance, promote youth participation in local politics, and so much more. Just imagine what your students will do if you give them license and drive to make a change in the world!

Audiences and Stakeholders

How frequently do your students get to engage with people outside the classroom? How frequently do they feel that what they create in school is more than just school work, that it has *real* value? Find relevant stakeholders for the work your students do, and bring them into the classroom. You'd be surprised how many industry professionals are out there just waiting to be invited into a classroom—they know they want to support computer science education, but they don't know how. Don't be afraid to reach out to the people in your community who might be connected, even tangentially, to the work that your students are doing. Not only will it help your students to see the value of their work, it will also let the world see the great things that are happening in your classroom!

Selecting the Right Tool for the Job

So you want to teach coding in your class, but how on Earth do you pick from the myriad tools available? Which is the "right" language to teach computer science in middle school? How important is it to pick a language used in the "real" world? Your neighbor's cousin's niece told you that if you aren't coding in C++, you're not really coding–is that true?

There are many questions to face when choosing a computer science teaching tool—and even more people out there with opinionated, even dogmatic, answers to those questions. There is no one "right" tool for teaching computer science or programming, no more than there is one "right" tool for use in the real world. Each tool reflects a different balance of goals, priorities, tradeoffs, and expectations. Each school, each classroom, each type of instruction or application will tip the scales in one direction or the other, but just as there is no one "right" tool, neither is there a "wrong" tool. While your choice of tool can certainly make your life easier or harder, it's not the end of the world if you and your students decide you've chosen the wrong tool for the job. As with everything in computer science, failure is part of the gig. We can learn as much, if not more, from our failures as our successes.

With that in mind, let's put off some of these big questions for the moment. Before we dig into what tools we want, or what we want them to do for middle-school students, it might be useful to disambiguate what we mean by *tool* in the first place.

What's in a Tool

Throughout this book, I use the word *tool* to mean some combination of a programming language, an environment in which to program, and possibly some libraries of code that make programming specific types of things easier. This is made more complicated by the fact that some programming languages only exist within the context of the programming environment, and some programming environments have specific libraries already included. Let's look at two examples in an attempt to make this more concrete.

Scratch is an example of a language and environment that are inseparable. It refers to both the blocks used to write programs and the environment in which we write (including the Sprite editor, the Stage, and everything else).

Python, on the other hand, is strictly a programming language. You can write Python using any number of different environments, from simple plain-text editors such as Notepad, to more robust environments that include tools for debugging, managing libraries, and publishing programs.

So, when you see the word *tool* in reference to programing, know that the tool you choose that may be an all-in-one tool like Scratch, a combination of tools such as those you would need to program in Python, or something in the middle.

The Tradeoffs in Middle School

Blocks versus Text

Many programming environments designed for beginners, including the ever-popular Scratch and Google's Blockly, utilize a block-based programming language, which allows for programs to be constructed using Legolike blocks that click together. There's a growing body of work researching how these languages impact a student's computer science learning, including impacts on conceptual understanding, self-efficacy, and ability to create. (Weintrop & Wilensky, 2017) Block-based programming languages solve three big problems for new programmers. First is the issue of syntax. The *syntax* of a language is essentially its grammar—the rules that dictate how code should be constructed. In many traditional languages, this includes things like when and how to use curly braces and semicolons; in others, syntax can be dictated by indentation and white space. The hurdle of learning a language's syntax at the same time as learning the basic logic of programming can be daunting for new students. It can be particularly difficult to determine whether bugs in a program come from a misunderstanding of the high-level logic or from syntactically incorrect application of sound logic. Graphical blocks have the syntax included, and they can only click together in syntactically appropriate ways. This allows students to first learn to break down problems logically and develop confidence in solving a problem programmatically before worrying about getting the syntax right.

Second, blocks support students who struggle with literacy and the mechanics of typing, particularly younger students. Typing and spelling can be practically eliminated by using blocks. Block-based languages typically communicate with both shape and color, in addition to text, providing additional hints to a student reading or composing code.

Finally, block-based languages are naturally self-documenting. Because they typically drag blocks out from a selection of all available blocks, students are able to easily discover new commands or functionality of the language. This feature is not exclusive to blocks, as many text-based languages include easily accessible documentation, but the act of consistently dragging blocks out to compose programs reinforces the location of documentation in a way that text-based languages do not.

These affordances that block-based languages provide to beginning programmers make them useful beyond K–12 education. Increasingly, these tools are finding purchase in industries where workers without computer science experience are needing to do some amount of programming as their jobs evolve (Weintrop, Shepherd, Francis, & Franklin, 2017).

Blocks are not, however, the be-all and end-all. Older students in particular find that, while block-based languages may be easier to program, they tend to feel less efficient, powerful, and "real" as one's skill grows grows (Weintrop & Wilensky, 2015). If students are equipped to program in a text-based language, they'll find many tasks that are trivial in text (like copy/paste, find-and-replace, and so on) are laborious, sometimes even impossible, using blocks. Despite the power and high-ceiling of many block-based tools, older students still report that these tools feel less authentic and less powerful than text-based languages. Students who have found success with block-based languages in earlier grades will likely find themselves ready, even eager, to transition to text in middle school.

Web-Based versus Installed

This tradeoff has less to do with how students learn, and more to do with the practicalities of your classroom. If your district is anything like mine was, just the thought of getting the IT staff to install software on student computers is enough to terrify you. Some languages require complicated multipart installations, which can complicate things even further.

The alternative is to rely on tools that are solely web-based because they don't require intervention from IT staff. While this may seem like the ideal situation, using a web-based tool can be difficult in districts where the internet is less reliable.

Language Tradeoffs

Finally, there's the question of tradeoffs inherent in each language. No single programming language does everything (or at least does everything well for a beginner). When choosing a language, you should first ask what you want your students to do, learn, and create. Some languages are more efficient when it comes to parsing natural language (such as Python). If you want to program Android apps, you'll want to use Java or App Inventor. If you want to program interactive websites, it's hard to pass up JavaScript. I won't attempt to articulate all of these trade-offs here (nor will I pretend to know them all), but suffice to say the choice of language is an important deciding factor that will impact *how* you teach and *what* students are able to create. Put another way, knowing what you you want students to create plays a major role in determining the best language to use.

Introduction to App Lab

To balance these various needs in a way that works across multiple contexts, this book focuses on JavaScript (the language) in App Lab (the environment *and* related libraries). While this isn't necessarily the perfect choice for all solutions, it is a good general starting point for many types of programming in many contexts. Moreover, JavaScript is a language supported by all modern web browsers; it is easily accessible without requiring additional software installation. We'll use App Lab for all projects in this book for the sake of consistency, and to help you see different assets of a single tool across multiple projects. You may, after planning your own computer science integration, find that a different tool strikes a better balance for your needs, but the core idea of each project can work in multiple tools.

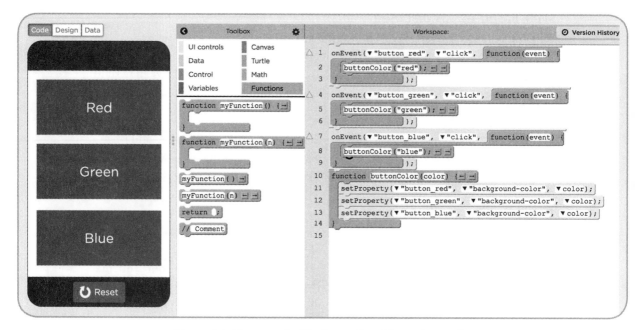

Figure 3.1: Program in Blocks or Text Using App Lab.

Working in Blocks and Text

JavaScript on its own is a text-based language, but App Lab has the ability to compose programs using either textual JavaScript *or* drag-and-drop blocks (Figure 3.1). The beauty of this approach is that students get many of the benefits of a block-based environment that we explored earlier, such as discoverable code and simplified syntax, without losing the power of programming in text. This is particularly beneficial in the middle grades, where students are likely to have a wide range of language skills and may want to rely on blocks for various reasons. Students in App Lab may choose to work in blocks or text, transitioning when they are ready or in need of the benefits of either interface. Even cooler, students programming in text mode still have the block library available and can drag in blocks for syntactically complex commands that turn into text instantly!

Varied Modalities

App Lab's primary focus is, as its name suggests, the development of mobile apps. This approach leads to a particular programming modality that relies on users interacting primarily through clicking elements and the program responding to those events. This is not, however, the only programming modality that App Lab can handle. It also supports Logo-like turtle programming, by using a sequence of instructions to move a "turtle" around on the screen. This turtle-style programming can be found in many different programming tools, either by default or with additional libraries, and can be used to create iterative art with a moving pen on the screen.

Designing User Interfaces

App Lab includes a Design Mode that allows for quickly developing user interfaces in a drag-and-drop style (Figure 3.2). Quickly prototyping an interface in this way means that students can spend their time developing the *logic* of their programs. Allowing students to develop their interfaces like this, without first worrying about the code, can help to reinforce that there are lots of roles to be played in software development, many of which break out of the traditional stereotypes of what goes into creating software.

Figure 3.2: Drag-and-drop design mode in App Lab.

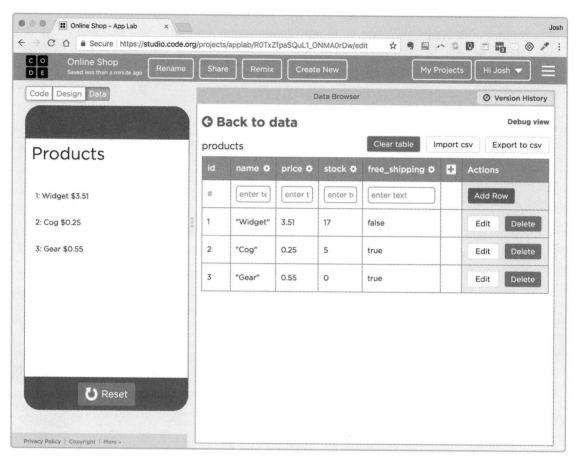

Figure 3.3: Database back end in App Lab.

Storing Data

We'll barely scratch the surface of its data capabilities in this book, so it's worth mentioning that App Lab includes a simple database back end that harbors enormous potential for writing programs that collect and analyze data (Figure 3.3). The process of designing a database schema, running a database server, and connecting to that database from a program in order to store and retrieve data is a fairly involved, and therefore advanced, project for introductory computer science students. App Lab's built-in database tools simplify the process to the point that even the greenest programming students can develop programs that harness the power of stored data.

Sharing and Publishing Apps

Many of our arguments for teaching computer science revolve around the ways in which student creations can reach outside the classroom walls, connecting people and allowing students to communicate their ideas. None of this works if students can't share their creations in ways relevant to the larger community. The apps that students create in App Lab are built using universal web technologies, so they can be run on any device with a relatively modern browser. Add to that built-in tools to share by text, email, or social media, and you can start to see the potential for connecting students with real audiences.

Adapting Projects to Other Languages and Tools

As I mentioned earlier, App Lab is only one of the tools you might use to incorporate coding into your classroom. For certain types of programming or classroom needs, there are better choices available. Appendix C offers ideas for adapting each of the projects in this book to other languages or tools. Additionally, you'll find examples of these projects in even more languages on the website for the book: **creativecodingbook.com**. If you choose to stick with App Lab, see Appendix B for instructions on getting your classroom set up.

CREATIVE CODING CONNECTIONS: **Creating Artwork Using Code**

This project, developed by Carl Lyman, involves drawing a picture using App Lab code on a Canvas screen. The project uses two coding elements: comments to break the drawing into parts, and sequence for placing one line of code after another. This is designed to be a starting app using App Lab because it does not involve using design to place objects on the screen or coding structures beyond sequence.

creativecodingbook.com/resources/code_artwork

Coding in Core Content Areas

This section explores coding in four content areas: language arts, social studies, science, and math.

The chapters in this section include:

- Correlation to standards and connection to real-world applications.

- Unplugged activities that can be used as a computer-free introduction to the role computer science plays in each content area.

- A fully mapped out coding project designed to highlight ways in which computer science and each content area overlap in the real world.

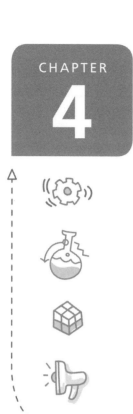

Coding in ELA

When educators ask me about integrating computer science into the broader curriculum, they are typically asking about how to integrate into STEM classes. This seems only natural; that *T* in *STEM* is a perfect fit for computer science. Though the connections between CS and STEM may be immediately obvious, the humanities provide a very fertile ground for computer science integration. In fact, when I started weaving coding into my own instruction, it was in my English classes. My first forays into coding in the classroom came by way of interactive fiction (think: classic 1980s text-based adventure games such as Zork, or choose-your-own-adventure novels). These early games came before we had access to fancy graphics and animations, so they naturally relied heavily on creative writing and narrative structure to engage the player. This kind of writing, which requires not only effective linguistic imagery but also writing in nonlinear narrative structures, was a new and different approach to writing for my students, and it engaged many students who otherwise struggled with monolithic writing tasks. The beauty of a nonlinear writing activity is that it *necessitates* writing in smaller chunks and iterating. It's not even possible to write from beginning to end when the story can branch out in myriad directions, which frees students from worrying about getting to the "end."

The Argument for Coding in Language Arts

Though the increased power of computing has allowed developers to communicate more through a visual medium, this particular kind of nonlinear narrative writing still plays a huge role in the development of entertainment today. Many modern video games require writers to develop multiple intertwining nonlinear story lines that can respond to choices made by the player. There are even filmmakers who have experimented with this kind of interactive storytelling to make movies in which the viewer has some control over the narrative.

Outside of entertainment, another growing field of computer science that relies on ELA is Natural Language Processing, which deals with the interaction between natural human languages and computers. Siri, Alexa, Cortana, and an ever-growing number of digital assistants have become an increasingly integral part of everyday life for many. Why use a keyboard, mouse, or touchscreen to interact with our technology, when we can talk to our computers as if they were people! But if computers are to every truly understand us, and communicate naturally, they need to be programmed with a deep and intuitive understanding of the language.

The idea of computers communicating in human language goes back to the 1950s, when pioneering computer scientist Alan Turing proposed a test for determining whether or not a computer had achieved artificial intelligence. In order to pass the Turing Test, a computer would need to hold a conversation with a human (via text) without the human realizing that they were speaking with a computer.

Developing programs that can understand colloquialisms, understand context to differentiate homophones, and adjust to our constantly evolving vocabularies are just a handful of the interesting challenges for a computer scientist with an interest in (and mastery of) language skills. Natural Language Processing frequently relies on the cutting edge of computer science, such as the field of machine learning. With a machine learning algorithm, instead of relying on the programmer to dictate all of the rules for a system (for example, the grammar of a natural language), they instead program the machine to identify developing patterns in data which it can "learn" from. As the algorithm processes more and more data, users can help to "train" it by identifying when the algorithm correctly or incorrectly identifies patterns. While this can lead to a system that responds more naturally and realistically, which often comes through breaking the traditional rules of grammar, it can also lead to programs that reflect and reinforce the biases of their creators. Take for example Microsoft's short-lived Twitter chatbot, which had to be retired after parroting the foul racist language it was fed by users (Wakefield, 2016). Understanding the existence and causes of such algorithmic bias is essential for a world where we increasingly rely on algorithms as assumed impartial arbiters of justice.

For our more analytically-minded students, this computational approach to learning language skills might just provide the engagement hook they've needed. If you don't love poetry for the art of it, maybe you can appreciate it as a tool for communicating ideas and emotions. Could you write a computer program that understands poetry in the way a human does? With the growing role of natural-language based human–computer interactions in our daily lives, I wonder how long before our language arts classes are compelled to teach this.

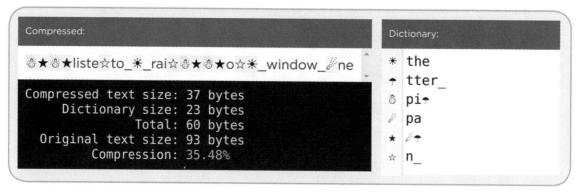

Figure 4.1: Text cxompression widget.

Unplugged Activities

Text Compression

CS Unplugged (**csunplugged.org**) is a fantastic resource for teachers looking to integrate computational thinking into their classrooms. The site collects offline, often kinesthetic, lessons and activities that engage students in a wide variety of computer science topics without needing to physically use a computer. These activities offer fairly rich computer science topics; they can engage students without any prior knowledge; and they can serve as a way to level the playing field when your students have widely varying experience and comfort levels.

One of my favorite unplugged activities from the series is an introduction to the concept of lossless compression, meaning the ability to store a certain amount of data in less space without losing any information (CS Unplugged, 2002c). From a computer science perspective, this has interesting applications both in the storage and transmission of information. The smaller you can make something, the more of it you can store and the less time it takes to transmit. This can also serve as an interesting investigation into the minimum required information to communicate with language. In this activity, students find repeating strings of characters, words, or phrases in a piece of text, and then replace them. If you repeat, one can substitute a much shorter code, which reduces the space required to store that text.

This activity becomes really interesting when applied to forms of writing that by nature rely heavily on repetition, such as music or poetry. Use it as a palate cleanser during a poetry unit, or anywhere that you want students to explore cyclical or repetitive structures in a text. As students work through this activity, discuss how much information is needed to convey the message. At what point does the compressed text lose its meaning? This activity is an example of *lossless* compression (all information can be regained after being compressed), but many compression techniques (mp3 music, for example) are *lossy*, meaning that some compressed data is lost. How much information can you lose from language without losing meaning? Find the activity here: **creativecodingbook.com/unplugged/text_compression**

The Turing Test

The Turing Test is a test first proposed in the 1950's by computer scientist Alan Turing to determine whether a computer can be considered artificially intelligent by engaging in a conversation with both a computer and a human. To pass the Turing Test, a computer would need to hold a conversation with a human (via text) without the human realizing that they were speaking with a computer. If the text proctor is unable to determine which is the computer and which is the human, then the computer could be considered artificially intelligent.

In this CS Unplugged version of the test, two students act as test participants: one student plays the role of the computer by reporting precomposed responses, while another student is allowed to respond naturally (2002). Two other students relay the responses to the rest of the class, which allows the first two students to remain unseen. The class then asks a series of predetermined questions of the two participants. Based on their responses, the class determines which is the "person" and which is the "computer." To connect this to language arts, ask the class for detailed reasoning behind *why* they believe each participant is either the computer or the human. Can they find clues in the construction of sentences? What about the vocabulary? Would they expect a computer to use poor grammar, colloquialisms, or metaphors? As a follow-up activity, you can have students develop a set of rules (or an "algorithm") for their own program that would respond in a more realistic manner. Though students at this stage are unlikely to actually develop such a program, or even compose a complete set of rules, they should be able to come up with a handful of ideas to make a computer-generated response feel more natural or human.

Find the activity here: **creativecodingbook.com/unplugged/turing_test**

CREATIVE CODING CONNECTIONS: **CS First Storytelling**

In this collection of activities, students use computer science to tell fun and interactive stories while exploring dialogue, setting, personal narrative, and more. Check it out at **creativecodingbook.com/resources/storytelling**

PROJECT: Interactive Fiction

creativecodingbook.com/projects/interactive_fiction

Overview

This project is a modification of the one I mentioned in the introduction of this chapter, simplified for ease of implementation. Beginning with a creative-writing prompt of your choosing, students will develop a nonlinear narrative—a narrative that forks at multiple junctures, based on choices made by the reader. While a more sophisticated work of interactive fiction might "remember" the actions made by the user, ours will more closely reflect a choose-your-own-adventure book, where choices by the reader lead to different branches of otherwise static text. An optional extension introduces the concept of variables as a way for the story to keep track of choices made by the reader.

Duration

Depending on your students' writing abilities, they will need one or two class periods to write their narrative. Once narratives are written, allow another one or two periods for students to develop their programs. If you have time, give them a day to share and play through each other's stories.

Objectives

- Organize and structure a narrative that includes multiple logical threads.

- Develop a simple user interface to navigate an interactive text.

- Write a program that uses event handlers to respond to user interaction.

Vocabulary

Event: An action that can be recognized by software, produced by a user or other software.

Event Handler: A piece of code that responds to a specific event.

Interface Element: An individual component of a user interface, such as a button, block of text, or checkbox.

User Interface: The part of a program with which the user interacts, such as buttons on a screen.

Teacher Prep

The first thing you'll want to do before diving into this project is decide on the context in which you want students to write. At its core, this is a creative-writing activity, and it really sings with a compelling creative-writing prompt. That said, this project is also an effective tool to explore nonfiction writing. When choosing a prompt, consider what role the reader will be playing. For this project to be effective, the prompt must lend itself to a narrative that the reader can navigate. Consider one of the following approaches to develop your prompt:

Second-person narrative: This is the quintessential type of interactive fiction. Students write in second person (referring to the reader as "you"), and the choices that impact narrative are made by the reader-as-protagonist.

Second-person debate: Similar to the first approach, but focused specifically on one character engaging in debate with another. This can be a particularly challenging kind of writing for students, as they need to thoroughly consider both sides of a debate and write choices that are both effective and ineffective in promoting a chosen position.

Third-person narrative: Less common, but still an effective approach to this style of writing. In this style, the reader is an omniscient observer and makes decisions on the behalf of any or all characters in the narrative.

Exploration of a location: This works well if you want students to work on expository nonfiction writing. The reader's role is to choose where they want to look, and the writing relies less on the nonlinear narrative and more on visual descriptions and effective transitions.

Warm Up --

Find a choose-your-own-adventure book and a simple interactive fiction game, such as Lost Pig (**pr-if.org/play/lostpig**), to share with your students. Engage with the story as a class, and allow students to respond to choices in the book or prompts in the game. Once students have a feel for the medium, discuss the following questions:

- In what ways is this different from reading a traditional book?

- How do you think telling a story like this is different for the author?

- What pros and cons do you see in this form of storytelling?

- If the reader has control over the outcome of the story, how does that impact the author's ability to communicate a message or point of view?

Story Outlining --

Introduce the class to your chosen prompt, and give them time to brainstorm potential approaches to the prompt as a group. Keep track of brainstormed ideas on the board.

Beat #1   Brief description: Introduction to main character

You awake in your roughly furnished cabin to the sounds of blue jays squawking in argument. The sun is already up, which means you're already late for work. You quickly throw on the cleanest-looking flannel from the pile on your floor and a pair of jeans still covered in sawdust from the previous day's work. You're late already and in serious need of caffeine. How bad would it really be to get to the job site a little later, if it meant you were a lot more awake?

Choice #1	Choice #2	Choice #3 (optional)
Work can wait. Put on a pot of coffee.	Boss said I'd get canned if I was late one more time. Better hurry.	Chew on some coffee grinds and get on the road!
Leads to Beat #2	Leads to Beat #3	Leads to Beat #4

Figure 4.2: Narrative worksheet for story outlining.

Once the class has generated a good list of ideas in response to your prompt, students can start outlining their stories. If your students know that this is a programming project from the start, they may be tempted to jump on the computer immediately, but *don't let them!* Good software developers *always* prepare before they start programming. The most difficult part of developing a compelling interactive story is the writing, not the coding. Students should get a first draft of everything done on paper before worrying about how it will be programmed.

On the website for this book, you'll find a worksheet to help students with the outlining. The worksheet breaks the narrative into "beats" and "choices." Each beat is a small chunk of the narrative that ends in a choice. Each choice leads to a different beat. The worksheet is designed for half-sheets of paper, with each beat on a separate half-sheet. This allows students to play around with restructuring their stories as they write them (see Figure 4.2).

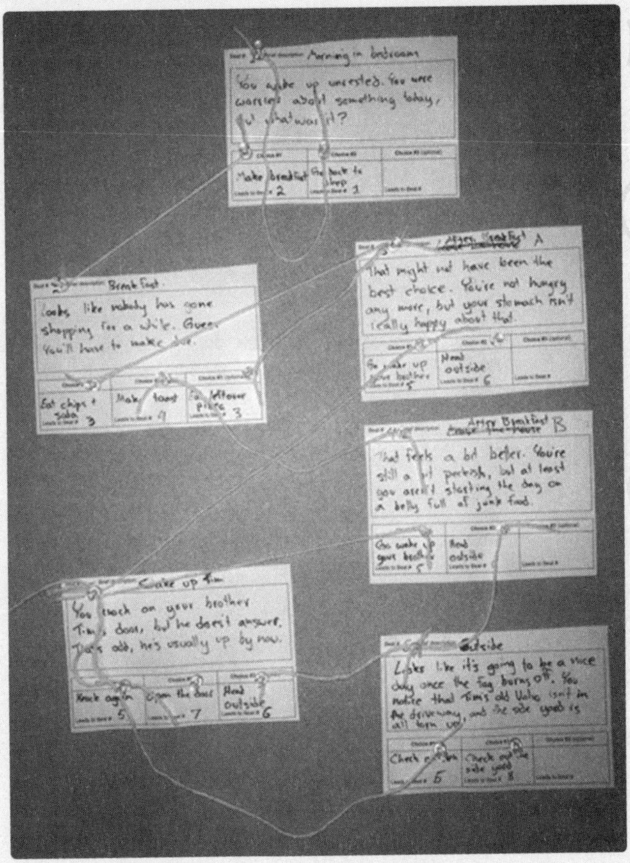

Figure 4.3: It can be helpful to lay out the story on a corkboard.

Using this worksheet, give students time to sketch the structure of their stories. The challenge for students is to consider the multiple paths that their stories could follow. If you have the space available, it's useful to do this task with corkboard, pins, and string (Figure 4.3). Each worksheet is pinned to the corkboard and connected with pieces of string. As student narratives develop, encourage them to think creatively about the flow of their stories. Are there paths through the story that might revisit beats, create loops in the story structure, or present multiple choices that lead to the same beat from different places? Encourage students to look for ways to leverage the unique affordances of this writing format.

Coding the Story

Once the outline has been completed, students can move to App Lab, where they will develop an app that allows readers to interact with their stories. For each beat of their stories, students will create a "screen" in App Lab that contains a title, text, and a button for each possible choice (Figure 4.4). The essential computer science understanding lies in composing unique and readable identifiers for each element and screen. While App Lab creates these identifiers, or IDs, by default, they are not reflective of content or intent, and therefore not terribly useful. When writing software, programmers must be thoughtful and systematic about how they name things to ensure that others (including yourself, in the future) can understand your intent.

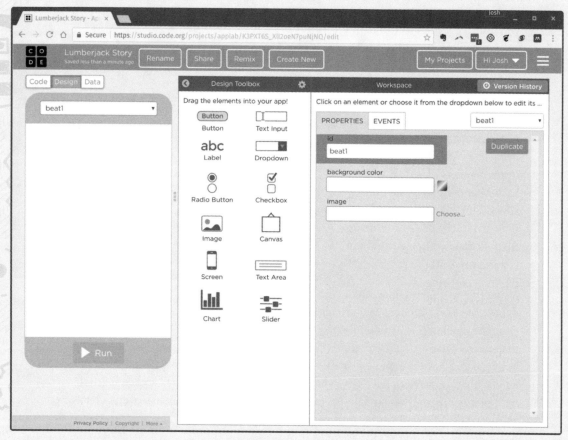

Figure 4.4: App Lab screen creation.

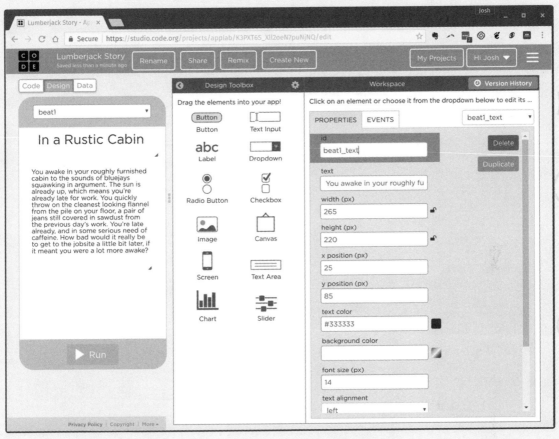

Figure 4.5: Entering text in Design Mode.

For example, students could use the beat numbering to give unique and meaningful IDs to everything. The screen could be given the ID "beat1" while each element of that screen would be "beat1" followed by a description, such as "beat1_title," "beat1_text," "beat1_beat2_button."

INTRODUCTION TO DESIGN MODE

Design Mode (Figure 4.5) works by dragging and dropping elements onto the screen to create a user interface. Though there are many elements available in App Lab, the only two that are required for this are the "label" element (for any time you want to put text on the screen) and the "button" element (for all of the choices).

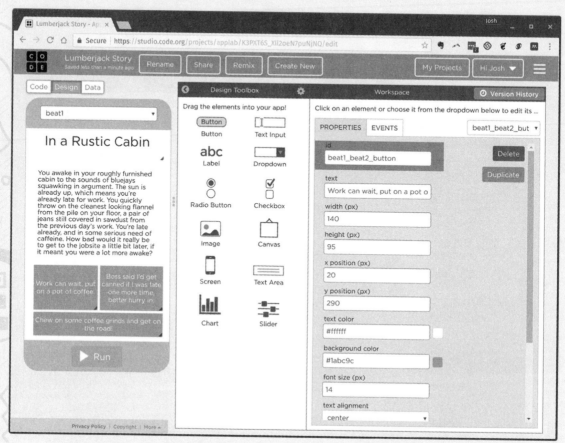

Figure 4.6: Adding buttons in Design Mode.

Each element has multiple properties that can be set, including its text, X and Y position, font size, and color. As students build their screens, they may find ways to support the tone of their stories using the visual elements in App Lab, including color, and even images.

PROGRAMMING INTERACTIVITY

Once the content of their interactive stories is added to App Lab, students can use code to link together their screens and buttons. There are two commands that students will need to complete this: **onEvent** and **setScreen**.

onEvent: The onEvent command sets up an event handler to watch for a specific kind of interaction, and then react to it. This concept of events allows us to write programs that sit idly for the most part, waiting for the user to do

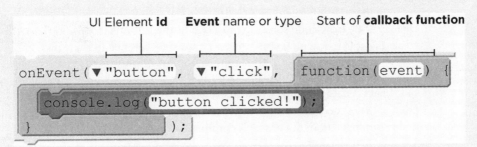

Figure 4.7: onEvent command code block.

something. Let's take a look at the onEvent block to learn more (see Figure 4.7).

setScreen: The second command in this program is much simpler than the first. The `setScreen` command takes a single input: the name of the screen to which you'd like to switch. It's that simple. For example, `setScreen("beat2")` would change to the screen named "beat2."

For each button, simply add an **onEvent** block to respond to a click, inside of which you can call `setScreen` to switch to the appropriate screen. That's it!

STARTER CODE
If this is your students' first programming project, they may find beginning with a blank screen daunting. One approach to scaffolding their introduction to this project is to provide a minimal amount of starter code. This starter code serves three purposes for students.

Naming Conventions

Programmers need to come up with a lot of names to use in their software, and without a consistent system for creating those names, it can be pretty difficult to read and debug a program. Good IDs are meaningful, descriptive, and unique.

In the starter program I've used a convention known as snake_case, where each word is separated by an underscore (making the name look kind of like a wavy snake). CamelCase is another common naming convention that programmers use. Instead of separating words, each new word starts with a capital letter, which looks a bit like a camel's hump.

It doesn't really matter which convention you use, but it definitely helps to be consistent!

1. Demonstrate how code *should* work. Two of the buttons in this starter code work as expected, which students can use as a reference in their own code.

2. Give students an opportunity to complete incomplete code. For example, the "beat1_beat3_button" event handler is missing the code to actually change the screen. By comparing incomplete code against the working code, students can deduce which commands do what.

3. Require students to code functionality on their own. In this example, each screen is missing a little bit more than the last, so by the time a student is working on "beat3," they have to create and program the buttons entirely on their own. At this point, a student should be capable of creating new screens and continuing programming on their own.

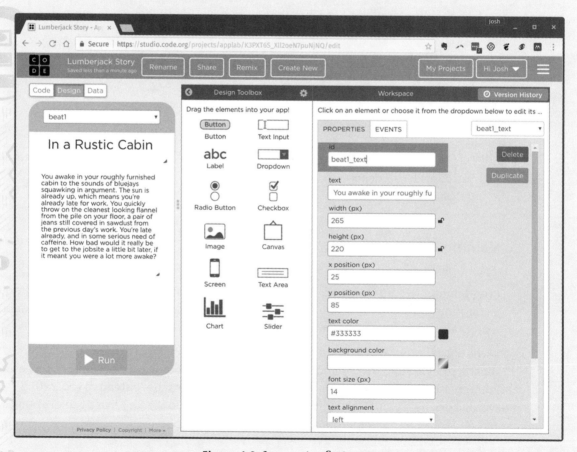

Figure 4.8: Interactive fiction starter.

```
// Choice buttons on ther start page (beat 1)
// Go North
onEvent("beat_1_beat2_button", "click", function() {
  setScreen("beat2");
});
//Go East
onEvent("beat1_beat3_button", "click", function() {
});
// Choice buttons on the blue room page (beat2)
// Go South
onEvent("beat2_beat1_button", "click", function() {
  setScreen ("Beat1");
});
```

Wrap Up

Complete this project by having an interactive reading party. Give the class an opportunity to play through each others' stories and celebrate the work. Consider providing a forum for students to provide feedback to their classmates. I'm particularly fond of structuring feedback in the form of *I like, I wish,* and *what if.*

I Like: One thing the user liked about the interactive story.

I Wish: One thing the user wished was different. This is a positive way to offer constructive feedback.

What If: One idea for improving the story.

If you have time, give students an opportunity to revise their work based on peer feedback. You could even have students swap stories to build on each others' work.

Extensions

This project can be completed with remarkably little code, which makes it a fantastic introductory activity for students without any computer science background. It can, however, be extended to better challenge students who have had some programming experience, or to introduce more programming concepts to students who are approaching this for the first time.

VARIABLES AND CONDITIONALS

Variables allow a programmer to assign a label to a specific value, and then reuse that value later on in the program. In interactive fiction, variables can be used to store unique information about the player (e.g., their name) or to record events that may impact the story down the road (e.g., if the user picked up an object that is needed to overcome a challenge).

Conditionals are essentially questions that can be asked with code, and that can trigger different actions depending on the answers to those questions. Combined with variables, conditionals can be used to change the flow of a story depending on more than just clicking a choice button. See the following code example, which uses both variables and conditionals.

Starter Code

```
// Use a variable to remember whether the
// reader has picked up the tool or not
var has_tool = false;


// When the reader chooses "take screwdriver and go to kitchen"
// Set has_tool to true and change to beat 4
onEvent("screwdriver_button", "click", function(event) {
  has_tool = true;
  setScreen("kitchen");
});


// When the reader chooses "fix radio"
// First check if they have the screwdriver
onEvent("fix_radio_button", "click", function(event) {
  if (has_tool) {
    setScreen("tv_fixed");
  } else {
    setScreen("need_tool");
  }
});
```

Standards Addressed

CSTA STANDARDS

- **2-AP-10:** Use flowcharts and/or pseudocode to address complex problems as algorithms.

- **2-AP-13:** Decompose problems and subproblems into parts to facilitate the design, implementation, and review of programs.

COMMON CORE ELA ANCHOR STANDARDS

- **CCSS.ELA-LITERACY.CCRA.W.3:** Write narratives to develop real or imagined experiences or events using effective technique, well-chosen details and well-structured event sequences.

- **CCSS.ELA-LITERACY.CCRA.W.5:** Develop and strengthen writing as needed by planning, revising, editing, rewriting, or trying a new approach.

- **CCSS.ELA-LITERACY.CCRA.W.6:** Use technology, including the internet, to produce and publish writing, and to interact and collaborate with others.

ISTE STANDARDS FOR STUDENTS

Knowledge Constructor: Students critically curate a variety of resources using digital tools to construct knowledge, produce creative artifacts and make meaningful learning experiences for themselves and others.

Innovative Designer: Students use a variety of technologies within a design process to identify and solve problems by creating new, useful or imaginative solutions.

Computational Thinker: Students develop and employ strategies for understanding and solving problems in ways that leverage the power of technological methods to develop and test solutions.

Creative Communicator: Students communicate clearly and express themselves creatively for a variety of purposes using the platforms, tools, styles, formats and digital media appropriate to their goals.

Content-Area Modifications

This project is easily adaptable to just about any subject area by simply changing the context of the story prompt. Some specific modifications follow.

Visual Arts — Instead of writing text, use the same structure of linked screens to create a virtual art gallery. Organize your art into screens based on style, and add buttons to navigate your gallery.

Social Studies — Make your interactive fiction into nonfiction (or historical fiction). Choose a culture, historical time frame, or country, and create an interactive experience. No need to stick to only text—include images to complement the text.

CHAPTER 5

Coding in Social Studies

The Argument for Coding in Social Studies

As with ELA, social studies likely isn't the first subject you think of when considering computer science integration, but don't overlook it. If social studies is the study of societies, citizenship, and history, then how can one ignore the role of computer science as a catalyst for cultural and societal change? Advancements in technology, particularly the advent of the mobile web, have fundamentally changed the way businesses, industries, and societies interact and problem-solve (Ala-Mutka et al., 2009).

Consider the role that Twitter played in the Arab Spring. In the absence of an open media, Twitter and other new media platforms expanded to fill the void of news, allowing people to communicate with one another and the outside world without being filtered or blocked entirely by their government (Khondker, 2011). Just as the industrial revolution fundamentally changed the structure of societies, and the roles many played in those societies, the digital revolution has already created massive cultural shifts. For our students to play a role in driving this new world forward, they need to be computer literate *and* computationally literate—to understand how to use the power of computers and the internet to effect change.

Many of the most socially powerful applications of technology, like Twitter, were initially intended for more pedestrian uses before being leveraged for something greater. There are, however, many programs that have been developed specifically to impact social change. The app Countable (**countable.us**) allows U.S. citizens to see when their government representatives will vote on important issues, and to quickly express their support for or against a given bill. SeeClickFix (**seeclickfix.com**) allows users to take pictures of public infrastructure problems, such as graffiti or potholes, and submit them to public officials. Apps such as these enable citizens to become more active and engaged in their communities, and they are the tip of the iceberg when it comes to empowering citizens to engage in their communities.

Unplugged Activities

Network Protocols

We may know how our local, state, and national governments function, but who governs the internet? You (and your students) might be surprised to learn that the internet isn't controlled in any meaningful way by a single entity; rather, it is governed by trust. No organization owns or governs the internet alone. All participants have agreed upon a common set of protocols that, as long as we all trust each other, allows the internet to function in a way that benefits all members. To experience this model of governance first hand, students can attempt to form a network to pass messages around the classroom. What challenges do they experience, how does this model deal with errors and failures, and how does this compare to more traditional forms of social governance?

The CS Unplugged activity Tablets of Stone engages the class in the difficulties of transmitting information across a network and the importance of a commonly agreed upon protocol in making everything function (2015). In a process that mirrors the actual internet, students divide messages into smaller "packets" and attempt to send them to an end user by passing through a network of other students.

While this activity only scratches the surface of how the internet functions, it's a fantastic jumping-off point to get students thinking about the societal implications of internet ubiquity, including information security, connection reliability, and even net neutrality. What if one member of the network decided not to pass your messages, or held onto them before passing unless you paid them extra?

Find the activity here: **creativecodingbook/unplugged/network_protocols**

Information Hiding

If you did the Network Protocols activity with your class, they may have noticed that there was nothing to prevent people on the network from reading messages, even if they weren't the intended recipients. The need to secure information has been around forever, but with the advent of the internet we now send vast volumes of information across a network where practically anyone could take a peek. If we were passing this information on paper, it might be more obvious that we need a way to keep it private. When it's all electronic signals, it's less apparent that we need to consider security.

How do you keep information secret and secure on a computer? What if you wanted to share that secret information with somebody else, maybe someone on the other side of the world? You need a form of encryption that prevents strangers from seeing your private information but still allows it to be seen or used by the intended recipient.

In CS Unplugged's Sharing Secrets activity, students attempt to calculate the average age of the class without anyone sharing their true age (CS Unplugged, 1998). Students encode their age data in a way that allows it to be used for the purpose of calculating an average without revealing the actual content. This is similar to the way in which you might send an encrypted credit card number to an online retailer. The retailer needs to verify that your encrypted number is real and connected to a bank account, but they don't need to have the actual numerical digits.

After completing this activity with your class, a natural follow-up is to discuss the role of government in information security. There are numerous examples of governments attempting to control the strength of encryption available to civilians, and even requiring that technology companies provide "back doors" to insure that governments have access to protected information and communications (Karsten & West, 2016). What are the costs and benefits of allowing everyone to secure private encryption, or ensuring the government can access information that might help it prevent crimes?

Find the activity here: **creativecodingbook.com/unplugged/information_hiding**

CREATIVE CODING CONNECTIONS: **eXperience Play**

eXperience Play, or XP (**experienceplay.education**) is an open educational resource that shows how to use Twine software to build text-based games that can engage students in digital storytelling and/or game design.

PROJECT: Apps for Social Impact

creativecodingbook.com/projects/social_apps

Project Overview

The goal of this project is to create an app prototype that addresses a social issue. This project can be used to explore societal issues in history, in another country, or locally. When choosing a context, make sure students have a variety of social issues that they might address using technology. The process of developing these apps is iterative and starts with paper prototypes, which makes it easy to customize for varying durations or access to technology. This project is less about how much coding goes into the final project and more about learning how apps are designed to address specific needs.

Duration

Plan for at least one full class period for students to brainstorm and come up with a social issue. Development of paper prototypes, and their testing, can be completed in two or three days. An additional two days will allow for students to create their digital prototypes. Provide as much additional time as possible for students to perform user testing and iteration, and to showcase student apps.

Objectives

- Propose a technological solution to a societal issue.
- Communicate the design of an app using a paper prototype.
- Design and test an interactive app prototype.

Vocabulary

Event: An action that can be recognized by software, produced by a user or other software.

Event Handler: A piece of code that responds to a specific event.

Note: This is an abbreviated version of much larger project. If you are looking for additional lessons or resources, visit **code.org/csd** to review the CS Discoveries curriculum.

Interface Element: An individual component of a user interface, such as a button, block of text, or checkbox.

Paper Prototype: A quickly made paper version of a user interface, used to test an app before programming it.

User Interface: The part of a program with which the user interacts, such as buttons on a screen.

User Testing: Testing an in-progress application with potential users to drive revision.

Materials

- Sticky notes
- 3x5 cards
- Drawing supplies

Teacher Prep

First, define a prompt around which students will design their apps. You'll want to select a general area for students to work within that ensures they have enough space to find an idea with personal relevance and that also addresses a topic relevant to your course content. Starter prompts could include:

- Design an app to address a major societal need in Victorian England.
- Design an app that would have improved the life of a pioneer on the Oregon Trail.
- Design an app to improve citizen participation in government.
- Design an app to make our school a better place.

Once you've selected a focus for the project, you'll want to curate a few resources to kick off the research phase. Depending on how much energy you want students to invest in research, consider partnering with your librarian or media specialist to support student research.

Finally, this project is most effective when students have real potential stakeholders to test their apps and provide feedback. Depending on how you've scoped the topics, these may be actual stakeholders or people who can role-play the target users. Either way, lining up stakeholders ahead of time can give your students an opportunity to test with someone "real" and provide an engaged audience for your students to present their final projects.

Warm Up

To inspire your students to start this project, share examples of other apps with social impact that have been designed by students. You can find plenty of ideas by checking out some of the larger socially impactful app challenges, including:

- Apps for Good (**appsforgood.org**)

- Congressional App Challenge (**congressionalappchallenge.us**)

- Verizon Innovative Learning App Challenge (**verizonfoundation.org/appchallenge**)

Pick out a handful of apps that you think will be interesting to your students and share them with the class. For each app, discuss as a class:

- Who was the app designed for? What kind of people might use it?

- What problem does the app solve?

Point out, in particular, apps that were clearly designed for people *unlike* the creators (i.e., kids). Developing a solution to someone else's problems can be a powerful way for students, especially middle-school students, to develop empathy.

Activity: Brainstorming

Announce to the class they can create cool and useful apps just like those they previously reviewed. Before creating an app, they'll need to figure out whom—and how—they want to help. To get a really great idea for an app, you'll go through a structured brainstorming process to identify opportunities. This process is inspired by the User-Centered Design Charrette from the University of Washington (Rose, Davidson, Agapie, & Sobel, 2016).

Place students into groups of four or five, and give each group a pile of sticky notes to use for brainstorming. Share the prompt that you've selected, and explain that you'll be brainstorming to identify interesting apps they could make to address the prompt. To land on good, clearly defined ideas, start big and gradually narrow your focus.

BRAINSTORMING STAKEHOLDERS

The first phase of brainstorming is to identify potential stakeholders. These are people who have needs that might be addressed by an app, within the scope of your specified prompt. Sometimes these will be the users of an app, but they are just as likely to benefit from others using the app. Each group should use their sticky notes to generate as many potential stakeholders as possible, one per sticky note.

Once the class has had an opportunity to brainstorm, collect all of the sticky notes and organize them into themes. Discuss these groups of stakeholders with the class, talking about how they might relate to the prompt or each other.

BRAINSTORMING NEEDS

With a solid list of stakeholders identified, groups can focus on specific needs. Let each group select a stakeholder, or group of stakeholders, to focus on for this next phase. If you can, ensure that each group is focusing on a different group so the class can generate a wide a selection of needs. Selecting a stakeholder at this point doesn't necessarily mean that's for whom you'll be developing an app. Again using the sticky notes to record ideas, give the groups five-to-ten minutes to brainstorm as many potential needs for their chosen stakeholder as possible. Encourage students to really get into the heads of their stakeholders as they brainstorm.

When groups have finished generating needs, gather and organize them into groups based on similarity. Discuss the common needs that bubbled up, and which needs spanned multiple stakeholders.

BRAINSTORMING APP IDEAS

Finally, using the brainstormed list of needs, students will generate ideas for apps. This brainstorming session can take a bit more time, and it doesn't necessarily need to be done with sticky notes. Allow each group to select a need or two from the last brainstorm to focus on for their app. Encourage students to think big here: How could we use technology to address, if not solve, one of these identified needs? While the focus is on the needs, make sure students are keeping their stakeholders in mind. Any idea should address the need *for* the stakeholder. Ultimately students will be creating an app prototype that will simulate their solution, but it doesn't need to be (and likely won't be) actually functional.

When all of the brainstorming is complete, have each group share their ideas with the class. If groups have identified ideas that they're passionate about, you can have them continue in the same groups for the rest of the project, or you might choose to use this time to regroup students based on the idea in which they are most interested.

Activity: Paper Prototyping

Before software developers invest too much time working on a new idea, they like to test their theories and assumptions in a way that allows for quick iteration. One approach they use is the creation of paper prototypes—roughly designed paper versions of app ideas. By quickly whipping out a design on paper, developers can test their assumptions and make changes before spending time programming something that might not ultimately be useful.

Using 3x5 cards to represent the apps' different screens, teams will create paper prototypes of their app designs that can be used to identify incorrect assumptions, unclear interface design, or unexpected features. To ensure that these prototypes can be effectively recreated in App Lab, you'll want to introduce students to the available user interface elements in App Lab (Figure 5.1).

For each unique view in their app, teams will sketch out a paper prototype on a 3x5 card. Once all of the screens have been prototyped

Figure 5.1: User interface elements.

on cards, the team can practice "running" their program by clicking on the drawn screens and switching to the appropriate cards when necessary. This manual method of testing the prototypes can also be run with other users. As students test out their apps with students from other groups, or even people outside the classroom, they should pay close attention to what works and what doesn't, but also to how each user *expects* the app to work.

Wrap Up

By the end of this project, teams will be well on their way to potentially useful and socially impactful apps. Give them an opportunity to share what they've created with a real audience. Consider having students develop elevator pitches, brief explanations of what their app does and why it's a good idea. You can then hold a *Shark Tank* style presentation of elevator pitches and app demos for other classes, parents, or potential stakeholders.

Extensions

Socially impactful apps are the bread and butter of many app challenges. Seek out some of the app challenges from the warm up or, better yet, find a local app challenge where your students can submit their apps. Don't be intimidated by the challenge aspect; most of these challenges are designed for students new to programming, and many even have award categories for nonfunctional prototypes. Every year, Congress puts on the Congressional App Challenge, which would be a particularly appropriate venue to showcase apps designed for a social studies class.

Standards Addressed

CSTA STANDARDS

- **2-AP-10:** Use flowcharts and/or pseudocode to address complex problems as algorithms.

- **2-AP-13:** Decompose problems and subproblems into parts to facilitate the design, implementation, and review of programs.

- **2-CS-01:** Recommend improvements to the design of computing devices, based on an analysis of how users interact with the devices.

- **2-IC-22:** Collaborate with many contributors through strategies such as crowdsourcing or surveys when creating a computational artifact.

COMMON CORE ELA ANCHOR STANDARDS

- **CCSS.ELA-LITERACY.CCRA.SL.1:** Prepare for and participate effectively in a range of conversations and collaborations with diverse partners, building on others' ideas and expressing their own clearly and persuasively.

- **CCSS.ELA-LITERACY.CCRA.SL.2:** Integrate and evaluate information presented in diverse media and formats, including visually, quantitatively, and orally.

- **CCSS.ELA-LITERACY.CCRA.SL.5:** Make strategic use of digital media and visual displays of data to express information and enhance understanding of presentations.

ISTE STANDARDS FOR STUDENTS

Empowered Learner: Students leverage technology to take an active role in choosing, achieving and demonstrating competency in their learning goals, informed by the learning sciences.

Digital Citizen: Students recognize the rights, responsibilities and opportunities of living, learning and working in an interconnected digital world, and they act and model in ways that are safe, legal and ethical.

Knowledge Constructor: Students critically curate a variety of resources using digital tools to construct knowledge, produce creative artifacts and make meaningful learning experiences for themselves and others.

Innovative Designer: Students use a variety of technologies within a design process to identify and solve problems by creating new, useful or imaginative solutions.

Computational Thinker: Students develop and employ strategies for understanding and solving problems in ways that leverage the power of technological methods to develop and test solutions.

Creative Communicator: Students communicate clearly and express themselves creatively for a variety of purposes using the platforms, tools, styles, formats and digital media appropriate to their goals.

Global Collaborator: Students use digital tools to broaden their perspectives and enrich their learning by collaborating with others and working effectively in teams locally and globally.

Content-Area Modifications

The general idea of creating prototypes of simple apps can be applied in nearly any context. In fact, you could argue that all of the projects in this book are nothing more than specific spins on this core project. That said, there are many content areas in which this same app development process can fit quite naturally.

Take the same general concept, but instead of working from the perspective of a given time or society, choose a novel and a character to drive the ideation of an app concept. What would an app designed to improve the world of *The Giver* look like? How might one design a dating app for Romeo and Juliet?

Select a specific career in one of the sciences, and design an app to help those scientists do their jobs better. Make a gem cataloger for geologists, or a whale tracker for oceanographers. Use this to give students insight into careers in the sciences, or to drive research into a particular scientific endeavor.

Coding in Science

When integration talk turns to science courses, I'm often asked by teachers and administrators whether computer science is a "science" in the same way we think of chemistry, biology, or physics as sciences. It's a reasonable question, given that "science" is right there in the name. If we do think of computer science as a domain of science equal to Earth, life, or physical science, it might change our approach to finding space for it in the school day. While the National Science Teachers Association (NSTA) hasn't released an official position statement articulating the role of computer science in science education, NSTA Executive Director David Evans published a statement titled "Computer Science Should Supplement, not Supplant Science Education" to the NSTA blog (Evans, 2016). The statement was released in response to a number of related events, including the release of the K–12 Computer Science Framework, an increasing number of states allowing computer science to count for math or science graduation credit, and California Governor Jerry Brown signing a bill to teach CS in every grade. In his statement, Evans expresses concern about the impact of increased computer science adoption on science classes, with a particular focus on the fear that computer science courses may supplant traditional science courses in high schools, to the detriment of students.

The Argument for Coding in Science

While I am inclined to argue against some of Evans' positions, such as his defeatist assumption that there's no time in the day to teach new subjects, he does make good points pertinent to our goals here. First, he points out that there are principles of computer science included in the NGSS:

> Computer Science principles can be found in the NGSS. Science and Engineering Practices include developing and using models, and using mathematics and computational thinking. In the integrated STEM classroom, using the principles of NGSS, educators are working to seek out real-world, relevant, authentic problems that would be of interest to students and ask them to apply computational thinking to solve the problem using data analysis, visualization, seeking patterns, and computation. (Evans, 2016)

In support of this overlap, or perhaps even interdependence, between computer science and traditionally recognized sciences, Evans suggests that in K–8 we teach computer science within the context of existing math and science courses. The authors of the K–12 Computer Science Framework have attempted to articulate this overlap, and opportunity for integration, with a Venn diagram (See Figure 6.1). The overlapping standards are shared in Table 6.1.

None of this actually clarifies whether computer science *is* a science. Peter Denning (2005) explored this question from an industry perspective. He proposed that the two are inherently interconnected, if technically independent. While many in the computer science and science communities have argued for computer science to be considered a first-class object within the NGSS, the reality is that it is—by design—a supporting character (Bienkowski, 2015). For the purposes of integration into K–12 curriculum, I propose that we consider computer science plays a role similar to engineering in the NGSS. It's a set of skills and practices that are essential to the study of all sciences (to varying degrees), and a set of discrete skills and knowledge that should be taught alongside other sciences. While the NGSS may not consider computer science a first-class object that warrants its own science course, it *is* more than merely a tool for teaching the subjects. This is the viewpoint from which I'll explore approaches to integration.

Major Areas of Overlap

Looking at the K–12 Computer Science Framework's Venn diagram (see Figure 6.1), notice there are two major themes common to computer science and the NGSS: modeling and simulation, and data analysis. Sheena Vaidyanathan dove into this overlap in an article for EdSurge, in which she explored potential paths for teaching that mirror my own experiences (Vaidyanathan, 2017). When it comes to modeling and simulation, the NGSS explicitly calls out the need for students to not only *use* computer models to explore scientific phenomena but also to modify and develop those models on their own (National Research Council, 2013). Irene Lee has lead this charge, developing excellent resources to support this overlap in her Project Growing Up Thinking Scientifically (GUTS) program, which was created as an after-school program and grew into a classroom-implemented module called "Computer Science in Science," in collaboration with Code.org (visit the Project GUTS website at **projectguts.com**).

In Project GUTS, students follow a trajectory called use-modify-create with a number of different multiagent models to explore everything from chemical reactions, to predator–prey relationships, to the spread of disease. This process first engages students in using an existing computational model to explore a scientific phenomenon. Second, they explore the code that runs the model to understand the assumptions made. Once students understand the model as provided, they can make simple modifications to the code to add new behaviors or better address simplifying assumptions. Finally, students are able to create their own models, using those they've seen before as a guideline. This approach encourages students to critically question other scientific models they encounter as those models move from unassailable black boxes to comprehendible, and modifiable, abstractions with necessary simplifications.

In one of my favorite progressions, students use a provided model to study the relationship between mountain lions and rabbits. By analyzing the code that drives this model, students learn that there are many missing pieces that could impact the accuracy of the model, such as the relationship between caloric intake and ability to move or reproduce.

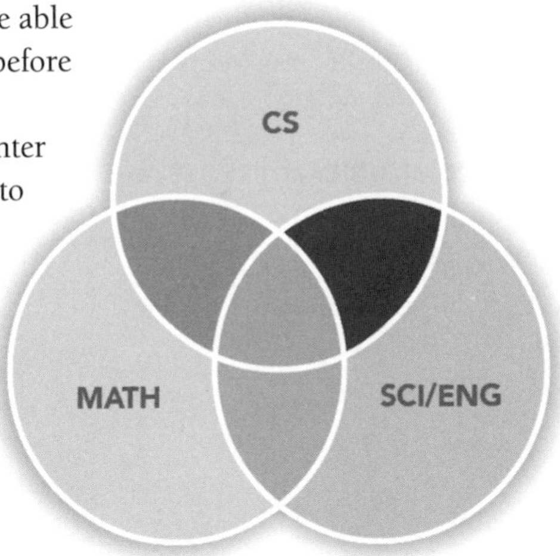

Figure 6.1: Computer science Venn diagram.

The second major area of overlap, data, is a less trod ground by existing tools and curricula. The role that data plays in computing will be an increasingly important component of K–12 education, particularly because of the ways in which "big data" continues to change the world. As we develop better and more accessible tools for teaching students to grapple with big data, I expect we'll find many opportunities to bring the real world of modern science into the

Table 6.1 Overlap of NGSS Standards Between CS and Subject Areas

CS + MATH	CS + MATH + SCI/ENG	CS + SCI/ENG
DEVELOP AND USE ABSTRACTIONS M2. Reason abstractly and quantitatively M7. Look for and make use of structure M8. Look for and express regularity in repeated reasoning CS4. Developing and using abstractions **USE TOOLS WHEN COLLABORATING** M5. Use appropriate tools strategically CS2. Collaborating Around Computing **COMMUNICATE PRECISELY** M6. Attend to precision CS7. Communicating About Computing	**MODEL** S2. Develop and use models M4. Model with mathematics CS4. Developing and Using Abstractions CS6. Testing and Refining Computational Artifacts **USE COMPUTATIONAL THINKING** S5. Use mathematics and computational thinking CS3. Recognizing and Defining Computational Problems CS5. Creating Computational Artifacts **DEFINE PROBLEMS** S1. Ask questions and define problems M1. Make sense of problems and persevere in solving them CS3. Recognizing and Defining Computational Problems **COMMUNICATE RATIONALE** S7. Engage in argument from evidence S8. Obtain, evaluate, and communicate information M3. Construct viable arguments and critique the reasoning of others CS7. Communicating About Computing	**COMMUNICATE WITH DATA** S4. Anazlye and interpret data CS7. Communicating About Computing **CREATE ARTIFACTS** S3. Plan and carry out investigations S6. Construct explanations and design solutions CS4. Developing and Using Abstractions CS5. Creating Computational Artifacts CS6. Testing and Refining Computational Artifacts

Source: K–12 Computer Science Framework (2016)

classroom, recognizing that practicing scientists are increasingly spending more time analyzing the data from experiments than running those experiments, particularly as we find more ways for computers and robots to deal with the manual work of experimentation (Wolinsky, 2007).

That said, even the ability to collect and analyze small data computationally can present a significant hurdle. The aforementioned Project GUTS ties into this quite effectively, as the StarLogo Nova environment allows students to not only collect, but graph in real-time, data coming from their simulations. Alternatively, we can rely on curated data sets from companies, governments, and other organizations to provide students with real-world data. The Awesome Public Datasets project (**github.com/awesomedata/awesome-public-datasets**) provides access to hundreds of data sets, many freely available, organized by content type. Some curricula, such as Bootstrap's new Data Science course, are developing new tools and techniques to bring data science to new computer science students in ways that can be incorporated into the study of science, but also statistics, civics, or social studies (Krishnamurthi & Schanzer, 2017).

Unplugged Activities

Routing and Deadlock

Throughout their middle-school science classes, students learn about different systems, from the cellular level to the systems of planetary motion, and beyond. The NGSS defines systems as crosscutting concepts, meaning a system has "application across all domains of science" and is therefore "a way of linking the different domains of science" (National Research Council, 2013). Despite the apparent importance of teaching systems in all fields of science, and using them to help students draw connects between different domains, there is one incredibly ubiquitous system which is left out of the picture. A system that we engage with daily, even constantly. A system which, though man-made, exhibits many of the organic qualities of naturally occurring systems. Computer networks in general, and the internet in particular, are complex systems with myriad interesting behaviors to study and connect back to other systems in science. One such interesting behavior is the routing of information from one point to another.

The Orange Game is a CS Unplugged activity in which students participate in a group simulation of information traveling over a network (2002b). Students are seated in a circle and given a letter that serves as their address. Oranges, labeled with those same letters, are introduced to the circle. The network of students must attempt to pass the oranges until all students have the orange(s) addressed to them. In the process, students will find that they have limited resources (hands), and if they attempt to work only in their own self-interest by holding onto the oranges addressed to them, those resources will become deadlocked and cannot be used to continue passing oranges to other students in the network. Though networks in real life are made of machines, they still need to balance the needs of the greater network with their own needs to ensure the whole system continues working.

Find the activity here: **creativecodingbook.com/unplugged/routing_and_deadlock**

Phylogenetics

The field of bioinformatics combines biology with computer science by using algorithms and data to solve problems in biology. One key advancement that bioinformatics has unlocked is the ability for biologists to reconstruct phylogenetic (evolutionary) trees, which can be used to trace how an animal's current genetic makeup evolved from an ancestor.

This CS Unplugged activity engages students in the process of reconstructing a phylogenetic tree using techniques from bioinformatics (2014). Though many of the concepts in this activity delve into topics typically introduced in higher-level math or science courses, the activity is designed for students as young as ten, and it can be used as a hands-on introduction to these concepts without requiring a great deal of prior knowledge. Using a list of words to stand in for the nucleotide bases, students play a game of "telephone,"—attempting to communicate a predetermined combination of words. Students record what they hear as they pass the message along, which leaves the class with record of how the message evolved through the game. By the end of the activity students will have used phylogenetics to reconstruct the evolutionary path of their game of telephone.

Find the activity here: **creativecodingbook.com/unplugged/phylogenetics**

CREATIVE CODING CONNECTIONS: **Project GUTS**

Project GUTS offers a middle school science program consisting of four instructional modules and professional development for the integration of computer science concepts into science classrooms through computer modeling and simulation.

projectguts.org

PROJECT: Lab Buddy

creativecodingbook.com/projects/lab_buddy

Overview

While we can certainly use App Lab to develop simple scientific models for study, it's not the ideal tool for developing models and simulations. Instead, rely on one of its cooler features—a simple-to-use database back end—to create a "lab buddy" app that mimics how real scientists might use programming to assist the gathering, processing, and display of data from a scientific experiment.

This project is a little bit different than the others, in that everyone uses the same app while gathering data from a science experiment. This is the most complicated program presented in this book, but students aren't required to do most (if any) of the programming. Borrowing from the use-modify-create method, students explore an example app to understand how it works before figuring out any necessary modifications for your chosen experiment. If modifications are necessary, they will be made by the teacher, with student assistance, beforehand.

Using this modified version of the sample app to record data, the class completes an experiment. Once the experiment is finished, they can export all of that data for basic analysis either in a separate App Lab app or a spreadsheet tool like Google Sheets or Microsoft Excel. Though the experiment won't produce big-data levels of data, it will certainly generate more than any one student would in an experiment, and it will be distributed in a fashion similar to how real big data is sourced!

Duration

If you do the entirety of this project, you should budget a day for students to get their hands dirty with App Lab, a day to run the experiment, and a day or two to analyze the data. To shorten the project, you can potentially eliminate the initial App Lab activity and have students use the shared app to gather data during the experiment, but then you lose any understanding of how the program functions or can be modified.

Objectives

- Gather a large volume of data with the aid of a computational tool.

- Summarize a large volume of data using a computational tool.

Vocabulary

Big Data: Extremely large data sets that, through computational analysis, can reveal trends and patterns.

Database: A structured set of data that can be written to, and read by, a program.

Object: In JavaScript, a type of variable that represents a collection of values.

Teacher Prep

The key to making this project effective is finding the right experiment to use for the data collection. You can use existing experiments you already teach, but you may need to reconsider the details to ensure that the type of data you're asking students to collect is both easy to collect in App Lab and lends itself to simple analysis through summarizing values. A good experiment for this might involve recording data that are:

- not dependent on time as factor in data collection (this makes it more difficult to summarize data across different students);

- easily categorized as a distinct set of values (e.g., the precipitate is red, blue, or green); or

- easily represented as a numeric value (e.g., temperature, pH, duration of reaction).

For the example app, I assume that students are measuring a single value across multiple specimens, such as the pH value of a series of liquids. You can increase the power and difficulty of this project by measuring multiple values.

Warm Up

- **Prompt:** Raise your hand if you've ever seen an ad on a website that seemed like it was targeted specifically at you. Maybe it was something for which you had recently searched, or a band that you already like.

- **Discuss:** How do websites know what ads to show to *you*?

Everything you do on the internet generates data about you—the sites you visit, ads you click on, even your location on Earth when you connect to the internet. This massive collection of data from computer users is known as *big data*, and by analyzing this big data, companies who don't actually know who you are can make a pretty good prediction about what you'll like, or what you won't like.

Scientists also use big data to run experiments on a massive scale to solve extremely large problems, such as decoding the human genome or searching for extraterrestrial life.

Activity 1: Modifying the App

Announce to the class that they're going to run an experiment today, but instead of everyone taking their own readings and analyzing only what they gathered, they're going to take a lead from the internet and gather big data (or maybe "medium data") by making a program that collects all of our data in one central location, which we can use later to analyze results.

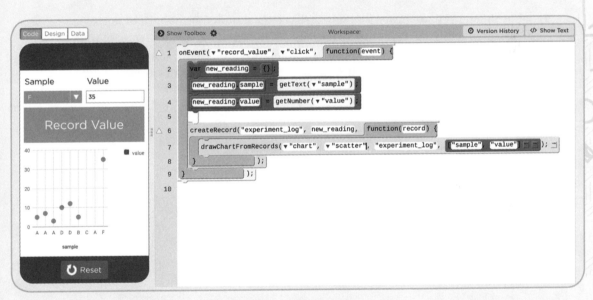

Figure 6.2: Lab Buddy starter code.

Remixing

Remixing is the act of taking an existing work, making your own copy, and then modifying the copy to meet your needs. In App Lab, you can create a remix by first viewing the code, and then clicking the Remix button.

Create a remix of the Lab Buddy starter project and share it with your students. Give them a chance to experiment with the program, entering whatever false data they wish. As students explore the app, ask them to consider the following questions:

- What happens when you press the Record Value button?
- What does the chart at the bottom display?
- How could you change the chart so that it is more useful or meaningful?

Ask the class to share their thoughts about the preceding prompts. They should have noticed that when they clicked Record Value it added their data to the chart, but also that the chart contained data from other sources (the rest of the class). They likely found the chart meaningless as-is, but maybe adding a different type of visual, categorization, or filtering would make it more useful.

At this point, you can reveal the code that's running under the hood, and potentially start modifying it for your own needs. Have each study make a remix of your project by clicking the View Code and then Remix buttons. Give students a chance to read through the code on their own, and then walk through it as a class:

```
onEvent("record_value", "click", function(event) {
  var new_reading = {};
  new_reading.sample = getText("sample");
  new_reading.value = getNumber("value");

  createRecord("experiment_log", new_reading, function(record) {
    drawChartFromRecords("chart", "scatter", "experiment_log",
    ["sample", "value"]);
  });
});
```

- The main **onEvent()** block responds to the user clicking on the button with ID "record_value".

- The variable **new_reading** is an object that will let users collect multiple values in one variable that can be saved to our database.

- The property **new_reading.sample** adds the text in the dropdown with ID "sample" to the object **new_reading**.

- The property **new_reading.value** adds the number entered in the text field "value" to the object **new_reading**.

- The `createRecord()` block stores the content of `new_reading` in the database table "experiment_log".

- The `drawChartFromRecords()` block is run after the record is finished saving, and it draws a scatter plot using the table "experiment_log".

There's quite a bit going on here, and it's not essential that we completely understand all of it. The important things to know about this program are:

- It's going to store a new record when the button is clicked.

- We could add new values to that record by creating a new property on the `new_reading` object. For example, if we wanted to add a temperature reading, we could add a line that saves the entered temperature to `new_reading.temp`.

Now that you understand how this example app functions, you can introduce the experiment to your students. What are you going to be measuring, and how are you going to use this app to measure it? If you are comfortable, you can customize the starter app with your students. Together, generate a list of all of the things you need to collect, and then model on the projector how you're going to gather that data. Alternatively, you can make any modifications needed to the app ahead of time and have your customized app ready for students to use.

Activity 2: Gathering Data

Have the class run your experiment using the app you created to gather your data. For this to work, it's important that all students are using *your* version of the app. If you need to clear old data before running your experiment with the class, you can do so by going to the Data tab and clicking Delete next to your table, named "experiment_log" in the example app (Figure 6.3).

If you open up the Data tab while students are using your app, you'll see new rows added in real time as new values are recorded (Figure 6.4). You can put this up on the projector so that students can see how all of their data is being combined as they work.

Activity 3: Analyzing Data

With your data collected, you'll need to decide how you want students to process it. Regardless of the tool they're going to use, you'll need to provide them with a copy of the data that was collected. You can do this by visiting the Data tab of your app and selecting Download CSV, which will give you a plain-text, comma-separated spreadsheet of everything that was recorded.

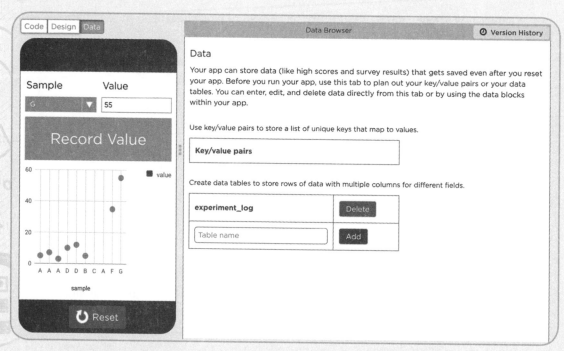

Figure 6.3: Managing database tables.

Processing with App Lab

If your students are fairly comfortable with programming in general, or App Lab in particular, they can process their data from within App Lab.

- Have each student make a remix of this starter app.

- On their remix, students can open the data tab and import the CSV that you generated.

- Have them modify the starter code so that the **drawChartFromRecords** command is using the column names that you defined in your app.

- Experiment with the different visualization options available. in **drawChartFromRecords**.

You'll likely find that **drawChartFromRecords** alone produces fairly uninteresting results. To go deeper with their analyses, students will need to filter the data going into their charts. See the extension apps available on this book's website for examples of App Lab apps that filter and analyze simple data sets.

Processing with Spreadsheet Tools

A much easier approach, particularly if you already teach some spreadsheet skills, is to import your data into a spreadsheet tool. Have students import your CSV into your spreadsheet tool of choice, and use it to summarize the experiment data.

Wrap Up

The interesting question with a project like this is whether developing a data set collaboratively produced better, worse, or the same results as working independently.

Extensions

This project relies less on students writing code and more on using computational thinking to problem solve with data. You can, however, extend the project to incorporate more direct coding. See this book's website for different versions of this project that rely on different programming skills.

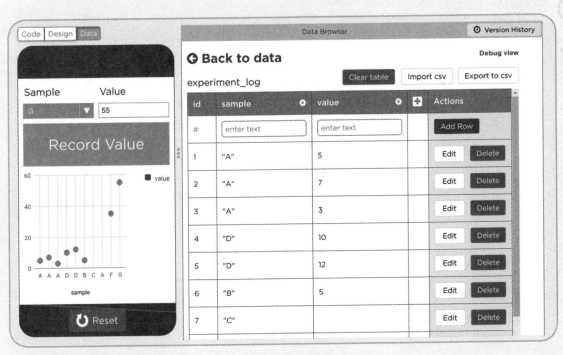

Figure 6.4: Lab Buddy data.

Standards Addressed

CSTA STANDARDS

- **2-DA-08:** Collect data using computational tools and transform the data to make it more useful and reliable.

- **2-AP-11:** Create clearly named variables that represent different data types and perform operations on their values.

NGSS

- **Practice 3:** Planning and carrying out investigations.

- **Practice 4:** Analyzing and interpreting data.

ISTE STANDARDS FOR STUDENTS

Knowledge Constructor: Students critically curate a variety of resources using digital tools to construct knowledge, produce creative artifacts and make meaningful learning experiences for themselves and others.

Innovative Designer: Students use a variety of technologies within a design process to identify and solve problems by creating new, useful or imaginative solutions.

Computational Thinker: Students develop and employ strategies for understanding and solving problems in ways that leverage the power of technological methods to develop and test solutions.

Creative Communicator: Students communicate clearly and express themselves creatively for a variety of purposes using the platforms, tools, styles, formats and digital media appropriate to their goals.

Content-Area Modifications

This is the most sophisticated app presented in this book, so when considering content-area modifications you should focus on keeping the core of the program the same, but changing the type of data collected to something more appropriate for a given content area.

 Create a simple survey for members of the school community. Use the provided app to collect that data, and then see what you can learn about the school society from that data. How do governments make decisions based on data they've collected?

 Once you get your data into a spreadsheet tool, use it to explore the difference between various mathematical approaches to summarizing values. What's the difference between mean, median, and mode? How do we know which to use, and what it might tell us about the data?

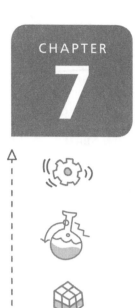

Coding in Math

Computer science and math are essentially the same thing, correct? Many of the first university computer science programs were housed in math departments, and some still are, so they must be closely related, yes?

Well, not exactly.

The Argument for Coding in Math

Programming can be a powerful tool for doing complex or repetitive calculations, and a deep understanding of math is important for many kinds of programming, including some of the more interesting specialties such as video-game physics, big-data analysis, or artificial intelligence. However, I'd caution you to avoid conflating the two. While many states allow computer science to count as a math graduation requirement, the National Council for Teachers of Mathematics (2016) has warned against such practices, arguing that computer science is not, in general, a replacement for the math skills necessary for college and career readiness.

There are plenty of types of programming that require no more math than one would learn in middle school in the first place (Sweigart, 2012). Given that many of our students already face math anxiety, and bring preconceived notions that computer science is little more than an expression of math, we should be wary of transferring the negative effects of that anxiety to students' study of CS (Wigfield & Meece, 1988). So, before you endeavor to integrate coding into your math class, you should first ask what it is you are hoping to accomplish. Computer science can bring the often-abstract world of math into the real world by giving students a place to apply math concepts in a meaningful way. Graphing arbitrary linear functions doesn't have much obvious use, but creating an app that uses a linear function to help me order the right amount of pizza for a party is a real tangible application that might engage students who may have shut down with respect to traditional math. Programming might just be the lens that exposes students to the creativity, expression, and beauty of math.

Seymore Papert was one of the earliest proponents of teaching math with programming. In his book *Mindstorms* (1980), Papert describes using the Logo programming language, which he helped to design in the '60s, to develop a microworld in which students explore geometry. Microworlds are domain-specific worlds focused around a specific context that allows for students to "learn to transfer habits of exploration from their personal lives to the formal domain of scientific construction."

The geometry microworld of *Mindstorms* uses a turtle as the primary object through which students think. By controlling the Logo turtle in a two-dimensional world, students can create geometric shapes and patterns, using their code to develop an understanding of how shapes are constructed, and even to engage with more advanced concepts, such as fractals and recursion, long before such concepts would be traditionally accessible. Simple exposure to concepts is insufficient in ensuring students are able to generalize concepts; the teacher must help students bridge their experiences in a programming environment and their traditional math curriculum.

The legacy of Logo can be seen in many popular programming languages and environments, whether they are direct descendants, such as Scratch and StarLogo, or any number of languages that support so-called "turtle graphics," including Code. org's Frozen programming tutorial. Even App Lab includes a set of turtle commands to replicate Logo-style programming.

The Vocabulary Problem

Before we delve any further into the integration of programming into math classes, we first need to understand the many ways in which the two are dissimilar, even contradictory. The potential for student confusion is high. If we're not careful by introducing programming into math while students are beginning to develop an understanding of algebra, it can be detrimental.

Variable

When you teach variables in a pre-algebra course, you might introduce them as symbols that stand in for numbers that you don't yet know, or perhaps you explain variables letters that take the places of numbers. With those definitions in mind, consider the following pseudocode:

x = 1

x = x + 1

In many programming languages, including the JavaScript that we'll be using in this project, that's a perfectly reasonable, even useful, statement. This is a common pattern used to increment a variable, such as increasing a score or moving an image across a screen. For a student new to algebra, this use of a variable might even seem to satisfy the definition we established earlier. In algebra, however, the second statement makes no sense. If x is 1, how could x also be x + 1?

There are two issues at play here. The first is *mutability,* or the ability of a variable to change over time. In math, and even in some programming languages, variables are considered *immutable:* once a variable's value has been established, it can no longer change. So even though JavaScript will allow us to change a variable's value, if we're doing this in the context of an algebra class, we'll pretend that we can't.

The second issue is what the = symbol means. In algebra the = symbol tells us that expressions on each side must be equal to each other. In JavaScript, however, the = signifies that you are *defining* the label on the left to be equal to the resulting value of whatever expression might be on the right. This is a nuanced difference for students, but if we consider our example, x = 1 can satisfy our definition of a variable in both algebra and JavaScript because we are defining the label x to be equal to 1 *and* we can say that both sides are equal to each other. The second line, x = x + 1 can make sense only if we think of the = symbol as defining a value, in this case using a previously defined value. In many programming languages, including JavaScript, it's useful to read the = symbol as "gets the value of," as in "x gets the value of x plus one."

Function

If variables are a bit of a stumbling block when it comes to reconciling programming and math, the functions are an utter quagmire. This is due, in large part, to the variety of different terms used by different programming languages that refer to similar, but not identical, constructs, including function, procedure, and subroutine.

The core issue is not that functions are *always* different in algebra and computer science. Rather, it is that in some programming languages, functions can behave like they do in algebra, but they can also break all of the rules of algebra. In algebra, we know a function must:

- take a specific range of inputs;

- return a specific range of outputs;

- always return the same output for the same set of inputs; and

- pass the vertical line test.

In JavaScript we *can* write functions that follow those rules, but we can also write functions that do things but return no values, or return different values even if the same inputs are used, or any number of other behaviors incongruous with the rules of algebra.

I don't point this out to discourage integrating programming into your math classes, but to highlight the need for caution. Unless you choose a language that also follows the rules of algebra (such as Scheme), there are language issues that you need to deal with explicitly, particularly if your students come to class having learned programming elsewhere.

Functional Programming

If you are particularly interested in teaching programming in a way that fully meshes with the rules of algebra, there's a programming paradigm known as Functional Programming that can help. Functional-programming languages use functions, in the sense that we think of functions in algebra, as the core building blocks of programs, and they also treat variables as immutable. While functional languages are less commonly seen in K–12 computer science, they are popular beginning languages in many universities as well as in the workforce. The people behind the Bootstrap Algebra curriculum (**bootstrapworld.org**) have done a lot of work in the area of programming in the context of algebra, and they have designed tools, curriculum, and pedagogy to teach algebra through functional programming.

Unplugged Activities

Binary

Computers rely on the binary number system to encode information at the lowest level, but why? What makes binary, or base-2, a better numerical system for computing than the more traditional base-10 system from our own youth? Understanding the role that binary plays in computing can demystify the 1s and 0s that represent the impenetrable mystery of computing in popular media.

Figure 7.1: Binary Game.

The CS Unplugged activity Count the Dots is actually a number of small, accessible, and hands-on activities that can be used to introduce students to binary using cards and dots (2002a). You can use this activity to help students understand not only *that* we use binary in computing, but *why* as well. Once students understand the basics of representing numbers in binary, they can use it to represent more than only numbers. Creating "secret" messages encoded in binary is a both fun and empowering application of computer science. If you want to dig deeper, hexadecimal (base-16) is another number system commonly found in computing. Ask your students to research where hexadecimal is used, and why.

Find the activity here: **creativecodingbook.com/unplugged/binary**

Once students have completed this activity, you can direct them to a binary game (Figure 7.1) developed in App Lab for further practice (**creativecodingbook.com/resources/binary_game**).

Minimal Spanning Trees

Finding the shortest or most efficient path along a network, or graph, is a common challenge in computer science, essential to everything from routing information across the internet to generating turn-by-turn driving directions. This creation of a path across a network of minimal total length is known as a *minimal spanning tree* problem, exemplified by the Traveling Salesperson problem. This problem, which dates back to a traveling salesperson's manual from the 1800s, asks the seemingly simple question: Given a list of cities and the distances between each pair of cities, what is the shortest possible route that visits each city and returns to the origin city? Though simple to understand, this is a computationally difficult problem to solve, and it is connected to discrete mathematics and graph theory.

Muddy City is a CS Unplugged version of the Traveling Salesperson problem, which allows students to engage with this computationally hard problem in a fun way (2002d). In Muddy City, students are tasked with building roads for a city; they must find the most affordable approach to paving pathways and ensure that each citizen of the city is able to access every building by walking on paved roads. Interestingly, solving this problem doesn't ensure that each person gets the shortest path from point A to point B, but rather that the whole community is made accessible at the lowest total cost, placing the needs of the community over the needs of any single individual.

Find the activity here: **creativecodingbook.com/unplugged/minimal_spanning_trees**

CREATIVE CODING CONNECTIONS: **Bootstrap Algebra**

Bootstrap Algebra applies mathematical concepts and rigorous programming principles to creating a simple video game, and is aligned to National and State Standards for Mathematics, as well as the CSTA standards and K-12 CS frameworks.

bootstrapworld.org/materials/algebra

PROJECT: Linear Function Machines

Overview

In this project students write simple apps that run a simple linear function based on user input. Though we are using a programming language that doesn't *require* us to follow the rules of algebraic functions, students are going to write functions that *do* follow those rules. These simple, single-function apps can be designed around most linear word problems. For the example program, we're going to use the following:

A new internet provider is coming to town, offering on-demand internet access anywhere you are. Their plan is to charge $8.50 a month to rent their device plus 5 cents an hour for internet use. They want to hire you to make a cost estimator app that would let potential users plug in the number of hours they expect to use in a month and see how much it would cost.

You can swap out this problem with something from your class textbook or of your own design. Whatever you choose, try to frame it such that students are being asked to create a real app to solve a problem for a client.

Duration

The core of this activity can be completed in one or two class periods. Further time can be spent writing more programs for different word problems, building more sophisticated functionality, or further developing the look and feel of the app.

Objectives

- Write a linear function to solve a word problem.
- Develop a program that takes text input.

Vocabulary

Function: A mathematical object that takes in a specific set of inputs and produces an output.

Variable: A reference to a value or expression that can be used repeatedly throughout a program.

Teacher Prep

To prepare for this project, you'll want to decide on the problem or set of problems and flesh out the contextual story around them. If you use my example problem, you might want to invent a name for the company, adding as much detail as necessary to make the challenge feel real.

In selecting problems for this project, I encourage you to keep the functions simple and linear, even if you feel your students are ready for a harder problem. You can always increase the challenge level after students learn how to create apps using a simpler problem.

Warm Up

Kick off this lesson by introducing the context in which students will be developing apps. Take the time to flesh out the story and get kids excited about making apps that have real-world uses. If you're using the example problem, you might introduce the challenge by saying:

> Hey class, did you hear that AccessNet is developing a new way to get on the internet, and they're planning to start a pilot program in our town? They've invented a device that connects to the internet from nearly anywhere, and they asked me if my students might be able to help them create an app that shows off how affordable their plan is.

Break students into pairs, and show them the specific word problem they'll be working on. Give the groups a few minutes to discuss the problem and come up with any questions they need answered before continuing.

Break Down the Problem

Once students have had a chance to understand the problem and ask any clarifying questions, they'll need to start breaking down the problem. As a class, work through the following steps.

REWORD
Depending on how experienced your students are with tackling word problems, you may want to model this more heavily or allow students to do it independently. Focus on stripping out superfluous information and clarifying the

known values, unknown values, and the relationship between them. Given our example problem, a reworded version might look like:

Given a number of hours, produce the cost of access with a base fee of $8.50 plus $.05 per hour.

IDENTIFY INPUTS AND OUTPUTS

Using the reworded problem, the next step is figuring out which values their program will need to take in (inputs) and which they'll need to return (outputs). Again, using our example problem:

Given a *number of hours,* produce the *cost* of access with a base fee of $8.50 plus $.05 per hour.

Inputs: *hours*   Outputs: *cost*

Writing Tests

Test-Driven Development (TDD) is a practice that professional software developers use that helps to write better, cleaner, and more bug-free code (Astels, 2003). Put simply, developers using TDD don't get to write any actual code until first they've written tests that make sure their code works. These tests initially fail, as they should without any of the actual code having been written, so developers work to make each of their tests pass. Once all of the tests are passing, they know that the program works. A cool feature of this approach is that developers don't really need to know *how* their program will actually work to write the tests, they just need to know what the ultimate outcome will be.

We're going to follow a simplified version of this model by writing a couple of test cases using simple arithmetic. We can then look at the patterns in our tests to figure out *how* the program should work. Once we've finished writing the program, we can compare it against our test cases to make sure it works as expected.

Based on the previous step, we know that the example program should take a single input of hours, so we'll write a couple of tests with different values for hours.

Example 1: 8 hours

$$8.25 + (0.05 * \mathbf{8}) = \mathbf{8.65}$$

Example 2: 11 hours

$$8.25 + (0.05 * \mathbf{55}) = \mathbf{11}$$

Notice that I kept all of the values in the in the same order in both examples. This becomes important in the next step.

Define the Function on Paper

Using the examples we've written, we can look for patterns that will inform our function writing.

$8.25 + (0.05 * \mathbf{8}) = \mathbf{8.65}$

$8.25 + (0.05 * \mathbf{55}) = \mathbf{11}$

Anything that changes to the left of the equals sign must be one of our inputs, while the value on right must be the output. Knowing that we can replace the test values with the names we came up with earlier.

$8.25 + (0.05 * \mathbf{hours}) = \mathbf{cost}$

Program the Function

With the pattern extracted from the tests, students can move onto the computer. If you want students to focus solely on the function definition, I've provided a starter program that has everything but the function finished on the website for this book. After remixing that starter, students should look for the function that starts on line 1. It looks like:

```
function estimateCost(hours) {
  return __;
}
```

This function, named estimateCost, takes in a single variable hours and will output the value of whatever expression is placed next to return. This is where we can use the pattern identified based on the tests.

```
function estimateCost(hours) {
  return 8.25 + (0.5 * hours);
}
```

Test

If everything worked as planned, you should be able to run the program and test it with the values you used in the two test cases. If your program returns the same value as your tests, then everything is good! If not, walk through the steps to figure out where the pattern used for the function diverged from the tests.

Wrap Up

Once pairs have their function working as expected, encourage them to use the Design Mode tab to "spice up" their apps. Maybe add Logo, or a description of how the app functions.

If your students have sufficient experience with writing functions, you may want to give them some extension challenges at this point. For example, I assumed in working through the example program that the cost would be prorated, but what if we instead rounded up to the next hour? Or maybe we want to expand the app to compare two different pricing structures.

Extensions

You can extend the base example simply by coming up with more complex word problems to solve, which will require students to add additional input fields to deal with additional variables.

Standards Addressed

CSTA STANDARDS

- **2-AP-14:** Create procedures with parameters to organize code and make it easier to reuse.

- **2-AP-17:** Systematically test and refine programs using a range of test cases.

COMMON CORE MATH STANDARDS

- **CCSS.MATH.CONTENT.8.F.A.1:** Understand that a function is a rule that assigns to each input exactly one output.

- **CCSS.MATH.CONTENT.8.F.B.4:** Construct a function to model a linear relationship between two quantities.

ISTE STANDARDS FOR STUDENTS

Knowledge Constructor: Students critically curate a variety of resources using digital tools to construct knowledge, produce creative artifacts and make meaningful learning experiences for themselves and others.

Innovative Designer: Students use a variety of technologies within a design process to identify and solve problems by creating new, useful or imaginative solutions.

Computational Thinker: Students develop and employ strategies for understanding and solving problems in ways that leverage the power of technological methods to develop and test solutions.

Creative Communicator: Students communicate clearly and express themselves creatively for a variety of purposes using the platforms, tools, styles, formats and digital media appropriate to their goals.

Content-Area Modifications

 Take any of the myriad simple calculations needed to build things by hand and make a useful app to calculate for you. Whether it's the circumference of a circle or the length of a triangle's sides, find those little calculations that are required to make something interesting and have students create apps to simplify their lives.

 Similarly, scientists have simple calculations that must be done on a regular basis. Even creating a simple random-number generator can be a useful mini-app to have students both create and use in a science class.

Assessment and Feedback

This final section looks at the practical aspects of bringing computer science into the classroom. It offers various approaches to assessment and student support and advice on what to do when things don't go as planned.

In this section:

- Rubrics and frameworks for use in assessing computer science projects.
- Strategies for debugging and teaching persistence.

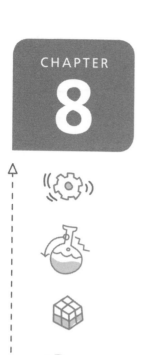

Assessing
Coding Projects

Y ou likely have systems and processes in place for assessing core content in
your subject, whether it's grading essays, weighting homework, or evaluat-
ing projects. When it comes time to assess the coding projects in your class, you
may need to reevaluate, or at least modify, those systems and processes. The first
question you should really be asking is whether you're going to assess the coding
portion of a project *at all*. After all, if implemented correctly, any computer science
integration into your class should be in direct support of the content-area standards
your students are there to learn in the first place. If you choose to assess the coding
content, you'll need to choose whether you want to give students feedback or
provide a grade for the content. Again, think back to your goals in integrating this
content. Is it important that your students' grades reflect their ability to program,
or is it more important that they get actionable feedback on this new challenge that
they undertook with you?

Once you've figured out the *why* of your assessment, you'll need to figure out
the *how*. A simple rule of thumb when assessing a coding project is to emphasize process over product. In the middle grades in particular, I want students to see
that I value the processes that they go through (e.g., design, iteration, debugging,
collaboration) over the final product. This doesn't mean that I *don't* value the things

that students design, but rather that it's less important to create the perfect app than it is to struggle through a challenge, try again, and come out on the other side having gained knowledge. Our educational systems spend plenty of time pushing the importance of being "right." Let's give kids at least one place where we demonstrably value persistence and don't demonize failure.

Developing a Rubric

To acknowledge the process of software development as equal to, if not more important than, the final product, I like to break my rubrics into two components: the first covers the practices that students applied in the project, and the second is focused on a balance of content-area and computer science concepts.

Practices

To help students see how they are applying the practices of computer science, select a few (no more than three) of the K–12 Computer Science Framework practices to emphasize in your project rubric. Some practices are more applicable than others for any given project, so look for the ones that you both want to help students develop and will be observable.

Practice 1. Fostering an Inclusive Computing Culture. This is a great practice to look for in the socially impactful app project presented in chapter 5. Look for evidence that students are designing their solutions with a diverse population of end users in mind. Make sure that you're giving students the opportunity to consider how their design choices may impact users with differing abilities and backgrounds. In this practice students should be working toward the following goals:

1. Include the unique perspectives of others and reflect on one's own perspectives when designing and developing computational products.

2. Address the needs of diverse end users during the design process to produce artifacts with broad accessibility and usability.

3. Employ self- and peer-advocacy to address bias in interactions, product design, and development methods.

Practice 2. Collaborating Around Computing. Any time you're asking students to work collaboratively, whether it's pair programming or larger groups, this can be a great practice to help students improve their general collaboration and communication skills. In this practice students should be working toward the following goals:

1. Cultivate working relationships with individuals possessing diverse perspectives, skills, and personalities.

2. Create team norms, expectations, and equitable workloads to increase efficiency and effectiveness.

3. Solicit and incorporate feedback from, and provide constructive feedback to, team members and other stakeholders.

4. Evaluate and select technological tools that can be used to collaborate on a project.

Practice 3. Recognizing and Defining Computational Problems. Authentically demonstrating this practice requires that students have the space to find and solve their own problems within the scope of your project, so it may not be appropriate to assess in cases where you're providing a high level of scaffolding. The linear function apps in Chapter 7 could be a good place to look for this practice, as long as students are finding their own problems to address with apps. In this practice students should be working toward the following goals:

1. Identify complex, interdisciplinary, real-world problems that can be solved computationally.

2. Decompose complex real-world problems into manageable subproblems that could integrate existing solutions or procedures.

3. Evaluate whether it is appropriate and feasible to solve a problem computationally.

Practice 4. Developing and Using Abstractions. Projects where students are required to identify patterns or develop programs with generalized reusable behaviors are good fodder for this practice. In this practice students should be working toward the following goals:

1. Extract common features from a set of interrelated processes or complex phenomena.

2. Evaluate existing technological functionalities and incorporate them into new designs.

3. Create modules and develop points of interaction that can apply to multiple situations and reduce complexity.

4. Model phenomena and processes and simulate systems to understand and evaluate potential outcomes.

Practice 5. Creating Computational Artifacts. This one is *everywhere*, but the details are what really matter. Consider how much agency students have been given in the design or direction of their artifacts before deciding to assess this practice, as it's important that students exercise a lot of control over how their artifacts are expressed. In this practice students should be working toward the following goals:

1. Plan the development of a computational artifact using an iterative process that includes reflection on and modification of the plan, taking into account key features, time and resource constraints, and user expectations.

2. Create a computational artifact for practical intent, personal expression, or to address a societal issue.

3. Modify an existing artifact to improve or customize it.

Practice 6. Testing and Refining Computational Artifacts. You need time for testing and refinement to happen, but if you're willing and able to spend this time, you'll be able to see evidence of this practice in nearly every project you teach. In this practice students should be working toward the following goals:

1. Systematically test computational artifacts by considering all scenarios and using test cases.

2. Identify and fix errors using a systematic process.

3. Evaluate and refine a computational artifact multiple times to enhance its performance, reliability, usability, and accessibility.

Practice 7. Communicating About Computing. Communication can take a number of different forms, depending on the venues you make available to your students. Sharing work with outside audiences, appropriately incorporating the work of others, or clearly documenting code all provide evidence of this practice. In this practice students should be working toward the following goals:

1. Select, organize, and interpret large data sets from multiple sources to support a claim.

2. Describe, justify, and document computational processes and solutions using appropriate terminology consistent with the intended audience and purpose.

3. Articulate ideas responsibly by observing intellectual property rights and giving appropriate attribution. (Association for Computing Machinery, et al., 2017)

Concepts

Striking the right balance of which content-area and computer science concepts you choose to evaluate is a personal choice that should be informed by the goals of your integration. You may choose, particularly early on, not to assess students on computer science concepts at all, or to only give productive feedback. I would encourage you, however, to use the standards I've identified in each project to assess at least a portion of computer science in every project, particularly where it overlaps with your own content. It's tough to make a compelling argument for spending instructional time on computer science when there's no evidence of learning because none of the computer science content is being assessed.

Check the website for this book (**creativecodingbook.com**) for some starter rubrics for each of the four content-area projects.

Alternative Mediums for Assessment

With a rubric developed, the final piece of the puzzle is the medium we'll use for assessment. Certainly you could just ask students to submit their programs and grade them as you would an essay, but that introduces a couple of issues. First, reading the code alone makes it more likely that we focus on the students with prior knowledge, because we don't get insight into those processes. Second, it can be difficult for a new-to-computer science teacher to comfortably read and assess code. To highlight a wider range of applied skills, and to save yourself the challenge of reading code, consider switching it up occasionally with one of the following formats, each of which reflect a practice from industry.

The Funding Pitch

Whether done as live presentations or short, prerecorded videos, product pitches are a fun way to model how a software developer might try to grow from an early product. In this case it's perfectly fine, even expected, that the product students have made isn't completely finished. This is an opportunity for students to highlight all of the work they've done to get where they are, reflect on what they'd like to do in the next iteration, and convince potential funders to get on board. Given enough time, you could extend this by creating a Kickstarter-esque crowdfunding page.

Developer Talk-Through

When bringing a new team member onto a project, developers often choose to walk-through a relevant section of the codebase, describing how each section works and what role each element plays in the larger project. Ask students to "onboard" you as a potential new developer by talking through their code, either individually or as a class. Encourage students to self-identify the weak points in their code. What sections still need to be worked out? What do you not yet know how to do?

Code Review

Software developers use code reviews as a way to get a second pair of eyes on contributions before they are committed to the whole project. Use this for smaller, formative assessments, whether among individuals in a group, or by passing projects around the whole class. The goal of a code review isn't to find everything that's wrong with someone else's code. Rather, it is intended to help you find the blind spots.

Supporting Growth and Iteration

All of the approaches to assessment outlined here are designed to serve student growth and iteration. I urge you to keep that in mind as you bring these assessments into your classroom. Far too frequently in education we view assessment as the end of the line, and our students have been absorbing that since early in elementary school. In computer science we never reach the end, everything is a work in progress, and we (students and teachers alike) would do well to remember that assessment is merely another opportunity for feedback to drive the next iteration—even if the next iteration is another project entirely.

Debugging and Persistence

Frustration is a natural part of life. In programming this can feel like solving logic puzzles, translating a foreign language you're just learning, or teaching a dog to drive a car. To survive inevitable difficulties when programming, you'll want some tools to build persistence and systematically hunt–and squash–bugs.

Setting Expectations

Computer science is a process of problem solving. If you can normalize the struggle and highlight persistence as a part of the process, your students will be more capable debuggers.

Don't be the class debugger; you don't want that. If students learn that they expect you to solve their problems. you'll be inundated with pleas for help, your students won't learn to debug on their own, and you'll become increasingly frustrated with each other (and that's a frustration we can avoid!).

Three Before Me

I introduced this as an instructional strategy earlier, but it's worth revisiting here specifically in the context of debugging. The phrase "ask three before me" reminds students to first seek assistance from tthe class instead of looking to the teacher as the source of all problem solving. Only after failing to solve a bug with the assistance of three other students may a bug be escalated to the teacher. This approach thins out many smaller bugs that would otherwise devour your time, while at the same time ensuring that you are aware of the more difficult issues students are encountering. Remember that escalating a bug to you doesn't make it *your* bug; it simply means that you will give it your attention. That may mean directing students to an external resource or another student whom you suspect has the answer.

Rubber Duck Debugging

I like to talk out my problems because putting words to a problem, particularly a big or abstract problem, helps me find little things I've overlooked. When my son was a toddler, he'd scold me for talking to myself when we were the only two people in the car. Pair programming can help to instigate vocalizing bugs, but sometimes you need a little something extra. It's one thing to describe your problems to someone who might already understand them, but it's more difficult (and useful) to describe your code to someone who has never seen that code—or any code. Enter the rubber duck.

Rubber duck debugging is a fun way to get students to talk through their programs thoroughly while diffusing the tension of debugging with a bit of whimsy. Keep a rubber duck on your desk (or replace the duck with your school mascot, favorite stuffed animal, etc.). When a student encounters an issue that wasn't solved with "three before me" exercise, hand them the duck. The student then must walk through their code, explaining what it does, and what the problem is, to the duck. Simply talking out the problem is often enough to unblock students, and there's no reason why you need to be the inanimate target of that rambling.

Debugging Tools

Many modern programming environments include built-in tools to help you debug your code. If you are using App Lab, you can read up on its specific debugging tools online: **code.org/applab**. Some of the debugging tools you might find in any given programming environment include:

Break Points

A break point allows you to specify a point in your program to break, or pause, the program. This can be a useful way to evaluate the state of your program at any given point. Are the variables what you thought they might be? Is the function you wrote ever actually getting called?

Logging Errors

The *console* is a place where your program might write error messages during execution, but you can also write messages to it manually. In JavaScript the `console.log()` function allows you to write messages to the console. You might use this to ensure code is executing in the order you expect, or to see the value of a variable.

Slow Down

App Lab includes a slider that controls how quickly your code executes, which allows you to watch things happen more slowly.

Traffic Lights

Successful debugging results in a big dopamine hit. It feels great when you solve a challenging problem. Don't deprive students the satisfaction and excitement of discovering a solution by swooping in with answers before they are ready. The Traffic Lights activity utilizes a color-coding system that lets students nonverbally communicate where they are the in the debugging process, as well as show others when they do (and don't) want help. Give each student a red, yellow, and green object. Plastic cups are nice because they stack, but you might also use colored cards or flags. When a student is displaying green, everything is fine. When students hit a roadblock, they can switch to yellow to show you (and other students) that they're working through something challenging, but they aren't ready for help. Only when a student flips to red should you offer assistance.

When All Else Fails

Sometimes we encounter issues that cannot be resolved with the tools available or within the time constraints of the class. That's fine; it happens to working developers all the time. Find online forums for the tool or language you're using, and see if anyone in the real world is able to give you direction. Write down the problem you're having, what you've tried, and what you haven't. Return to the problem tomorrow with a fresh perspective. The important thing is not to read too much into a single challenging bug, and to not lose confidence. You can do this!

Conclusion

B ack in the first part of this book I asked you to take a chance with me and take a step towards integrating Computer Science into your classroom. The activities and lessons I've collected in this book reflect the influence and impact of hundreds of teachers on my own growth, many of whom never actually taught a dedicated Computer Science class. By bringing CS into your class you're not only bringing an essential learning opportunity to students who may not otherwise get the chance, you're also doing it in a way that can expand all students' view of what CS is, who does it, and the impacts it has on society. Resist the temptation to "play" the CS teacher you - you are a teacher of computer science, and the unique background you bring as a content area teacher makes is a valuable asset. The work you put in here can lay the foundation for your students to become better prepared for living in the modern world, regardless of whether they choose to pursue a career in technology or not.

References

Ala-Mutka, K., Broster, D., Cachia, R., Centeno, C., Feijóo, C., Haché, A., . . . Valverde, J. (2009). The impact of social computing on the EU information society and economy. *JRC Scientific and Technical Report EUR* 24063 EN. Retrieved from www.ict-21.ch/com-ict/IMG/pdf/JRC54327.pdf

Association for Computing Machinery, et al. (2017).K-12 Framework for computer science education. Retrieved from http://k12cs.org.

Astels, D. (2003). *Test-driven development: A practical guide.* Upper Saddle River, NJ: Prentice Hall Professional Technical Reference.

Barker, L., McDowell, C., & Kalahar, K. (2009). Exploring factors that influence computer science introductory course students to persist in the major. *ACM SIGCSE Bulletin*, 41, 153–57.

Bienkowski, M. (2015). Making computer science a first-class object in the K-12 next generation science standards [abstract]. *Proceedings of the 46th Acm Technical Symposium on Computer Science Education*, 513–13. doi:10.1145/2676723.2691882

Buckley, M., Nordlinger, J., & Subramanian, D. (2008). Socially relevant computing. *ACM SIGCSE Bulletin*, 40 (1), 347–51.

Cockburn, A., & Williams, L. (2000). The costs and benefits of pair programming. In G. Succi & M. Marchesi (Eds.), *Extreme Programming Examined (pp. 223–47)*. Reading, MA: Addison–Wesley Publishing Co.

Code.org. (n.d.). Lab Buddy Project. Retrieved from https://studio.code.org/projects/applab/Sl2_d3hr00jNKTEmPblkAA/remix

Code.org. (2017a). Advocacy Coalition. Retrieved from https://code.org/advocacy

Code.org. (2017b). Binary game. Retrieved from https://studio.code.org/projects/applab/iukLbcDnzqgoxuu810unLw

——. (2017c). CS discoveries curriculum guide. Retrieved from https://code.org/files/CSDiscoveries-Curriculum-Guide.pdf.

Computer Science Teachers Association. (2017). K–12 CSTA Computer Science Standards. Retrieved from www.csteachers.org/page/standards.

Computer Science Teachers Association, International Society for Technology in Education. (2011). *Computational thinking leadership toolkit.* Retrieved from www.csteachers.org/resource/resmgr/471.11CTLeadershiptToolkit-S.pdf.

CS Unplugged. (1998). *Information hiding.* Retrieved from http://csunplugged.org/information-hiding/

——. (2002a). *Binary numbers.* Retrieved from http://csunplugged.org/binary-numbers/

—— . (2002b). *Routing and Deadlock.* Retrieved from http://csunplugged.org/routing-and-deadlock/

——. (2002c). *Text compression.* Retrieved from http://csunplugged.org/text-compression/

——. (2002d). *Minimal Spanning Trees.* Retrieved from http://csunplugged.org/minimal-spanning-trees/

——. (2014). *Phylogenetics.* Retrieved from http://csunplugged.org/phylogenetics/

——. (2015). *Network Protocols.* Retrieved from http://csunplugged.org/network-protocols/

Denning, P. (2005). Is computer science science? *Communications of the ACM 48*(4), 27–31.

Dweck, C. (2006). *Mindset: The new psychology of success: How we can learn to fulfill our potential.* New York, NY: Ballantine Books.

——. (2015). Carol Dweck revisits the 'growth mindset.' *Education Week, 35*(5), 20–24.

Evans, D. (2016, October 17). Computer science should supplement, not supplant science education [blog]. Retrieved from http://nstacommunities.org/blog/2016/10/17/computer science-should-supplement-not-supplant-science-education/

Gomes, C. (2009). Computational sustainability: Computational methods for a sustainable environment, economy, and society. *The Bridge, 39* (4), 5–13.

Google & Gallup. (2016). "Diversity gaps in computer science: Exploring the underrepresentation of girls, blacks, and hispanics." [Survey report]. Retrieved from http://services.google.com/fh/files/misc/diversity-gaps-in-computer science-report.pdf

Heinrichs, H. (2013). Sharing economy: A potential new pathway to sustainability. *GAIA-Ecological Perspectives for Science and Society, 22* (4), 228–31.

International Society for Technology in Education. (2016). ISTE standards for students. Retrieved from

www.iste.org/standards/for-computer science-educators.

John Walker, S. (2015). Review of the book *Big data: A revolution that will transform how we live, work, and think,* by Viktor Mayer-Schönberger & Kenneth Cukier. *International Journal of Advertising, 33.*

Karsten, J., & West, D. (2016, April 19). A brief history of U.S. encryption policy. Retrieved from www.brookings.edu/blog/ techtank/2016/04/19/a-brief-history-of-u-s-encryption-policy/

Khondker, H. (2011). Role of the new media in the Arab Spring. *Globalizations, 8*(5), 675–79. doi:10.1080/14747731.2011.621287

Krishnamurthi, S., & Schanzer, E. (2017, August 22). Bootstrap's data science course for middle- and high-school students. Retrieved from www.techatbloomberg.com/blog/ bootstraps-data-science-course-for-middle-and-high-school-students/

Lewis, C. (2017). Good (and bad) reasons to teach all students computer science. In Fee, S., Holland-Minkley, A., & Lombardi, T. (Eds.), *New Directions for Computing Education* (pp. 15–34). Springer.

McDowell, C., Werner, L., Bullock, H., & Fernald, J. (2003). The impact of pair programming on student performance, perception, and persistence. *Proceedings of the 25th International Conference on Software Engineering,* 602–7. doi: 10.1109/ICSE.2003.1201243

———. (2006). Pair programming improves student retention, confidence, and program quality. *Communications of the ACM, 49*(8), 90–95. doi: 10.1145/1145287.1145293

National Council for Teachers of Mathematics. (2016). *Computer science and mathematics education* [Position statement]. Retrieved from www.nctm.org/uploadedFiles/Standards_and_Positions/Position_Statements/Computer%20science%20and%20math%20ed%20022416.pdf

National Governors Association Center for Best Practices, & Council of Chief State School Officers. (2018). Common Core State Standards for mathematics. Retrieved from www.corestandards.org/Math/

National Research Council. (2013). *Next generation science standards: For states, by states.* Washington, D.C.: The National Academies Press.

Papert, S. (1980). *Mindstorms: Children, computers, and Powerful Ideas.* New York, NY: Basic Books, Inc.

Patitsas, E., Berlin, J., Craig, M., & Easterbrook, S. (2016). Evidence that computer science grades are not bimodal. *Proceedings of the 2016 ACM Conference on International Computing Education Research*, 113–21. doi:10.1145/2960310.2960312

Puentedura, R. (2014). *SAMR and TPCK: A hands-on approach to classroom practice.* Retrieved from www.hippasus.com/rrpweblog/archives/2014/12/11/SAMRandTPCK_HandsOnApproachClassroomPractice.pdf

Rose, E., Davidson, A., Agapie, E. & Sobel, K. (2016). Designing our future students: Introducing user experience to teens through a UCD charette. *Proceedings of the 34th ACM International Conference on the Design of Communication*, 22.

Sweigart, A. (2012, March 18). "How much math do I need to know to program?" Not that much, actually [Blog]. Retrieved from https://inventwithpython.com/blog/2012/03/18/how-much-math-do-i-need-to-know-to-program-not-that-much-actually/

Turing, A. (1950). I.–Computing machinery and intelligence. *Mind LIX* (236), 433–60. doi:10.1093/mind/LIX.236.433

Vaidyanathan, S. (2017, November 16). Why computer science belongs in every science teacher's classroom. *EdSurge*. Retrieved from www.edsurge.com/news/2017-11-16-why-computer science-belongs-in-every-science-teacher-s-classroom

Vigna, P., & Casey, M. (2016). *The age of cryptocurrency: How bitcoin and the blockchain are challenging the global economic order.* New York, NY: Picador.

Wakefield, J. (2016). Microsoft chatbot is taught to swear on Twitter. *BBC News, 24.*

Weintrop, D., & Wilensky, U. (2015). To block or not to block, that is the question: Students' perceptions of blocks-based programming. Proceedings of the 14th International Conference on Interaction Design and Children, 199–208. DOI:10.1145/2771839.2771860

——. (2017). How block-based languages support novices. *Journal of Visual Languages and Sentient Systems, 3,* 92–100.

Weintrop, D., Shepherd, D., Francis, P. & Franklin, D. (2017, 9–10 October). *Blockly goes to work: Block-based programming for industrial robots.* Paper presented at the IEEE Blocks and Beyond Workshop. Retrieved April 23, 2018, from IEEE Xplore. doi: 10.1109/BLOCKS.2017.8120406

Werner, L.L., Hanks, B., & McDowell, C. (2004). Pair-programming helps female computer science students. *Journal on Educational Resources in Computing (JERIC), 4* (1). doi: 10.1145/1060071.1060075

Wigfield, A., & Meece, J.L. (1988). Math anxiety in elementary and secondary school students. *Journal of Educational Psychology, 80*(2), 210.

Williams, L. & Upchurch, R. L. (2001). In support of student pair-programming. *ACM SIGCSE Bulletin, 33,* 327–31. doi: 10.1145/364447.364614

Wing, J. M. (2006). Computational thinking. *Communications of the ACM, 49*(3), 33–35. Retrieved from www.cs.cmu.edu/~15110-s13/Wing06-ct.pdf.

Wolinsky, H. (2007). I, scientist. *EMBO Reports, 8* (8), 720–22.

Resources

If you're interested in becoming a better programmer, I recommend you look into the following resources.

Online Courses and Training

Code Academy (**codecademy.com**) Self-paced programming instruction that walks you through building specific projects. While the activities do a good job of telling you what you're getting right or wrong (within the constraints of a given task), they don't do as well building the underlying conceptual understandings you would need to build something on your own. This pairs well as a skill-building tool alongside a more conceptual support.

Code.org CS Principles (**https://code.org/educate/csp**) While this is a high school AP course, it is the course for which App Lab was created. If you want to get a solid introduction to programming in App Lab, you'd be hard-pressed to do better than this.

Professional Development

Learning more about programming is one thing, but learning to become a better computer science teacher is another thing altogether. No online or self-directed instruction can replace high-quality, in-person professional development, but there are certainly those that can do a lot of good. If you can, find a well-regarded computer science professional development course to attend in your area. In lieu of that, check out some of these resources to better develop your computer science pedagogical chops.

Join the CSTA. The Computer Science Teachers Association should be the first stop on any teacher's journey toward computer science. Aside from a fantastic yearly conference, a set of national standards, and a resource-packed newsletter, the CSTA is composed of dozens of regional chapters that host in-person gatherings that can help you build a local support network. And before you say "but I'm not a CS teacher..." stop! The CSTA is for all teachers of computer science; if you're looking to tackle any of the ideas in this book, you're part of the club.

Join the ISTE Computer Science Network. ISTE has many active Professional Learning Networks (PLNs), and the Computer Science Network is a great place to find resources for teaching computer science and computational thinking while connecting with other computer science educators around the world.

Read the CS Discoveries Curriculum Guide. Full disclosure: CS Discoveries is one of my curriculum projects at Code.org. It's an introductory course for grades 6-10, and the curriculum guide is essentially its philosophical front matter. Whether you're teaching the curriculum or not, reading about how and why it was designed could certainly help you in thinking about your own instructional design.

Getting Set Up in App Lab

App Lab is an entirely web-based tool, which means there's actually very little set-up that needs to be done before you can use it in the classroom. The one thing you will need is to set up a classroom so you can track your students' work.

Create Your Account

Before doing anything else, you'll need to create an account for yourself on Code. org (**code.org**). Make sure to select Teacher as the account type so that you'll have access to the classroom management tools.

Create a Section

Now that you have an account and are logged in, you'll want to create a new "section" for each of your classes. When creating a section, the most important choice you'll need to make is how you want students to log in.

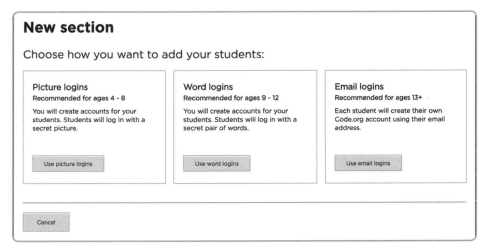

Figure B.1: Section login choices.

The three student login options work as follows:

Picture Logins: Designed for younger students, especially pre-readers, this option allows students to match their names with automatically generated pictures. If you use this log in you'll be creating accounts for your students, which can be done in batches by copying and pasting from a spreadsheet.

Word Logins: Identical to picture logins, except students have to type in two secret words after selecting their names from a list.

Email Logins: If your students have email addresses, this is the preferred approach to setting up a classroom, as students can easily take their accounts with them after they're done with your class. In this mode you get a special code that students can use to join your section after they've created accounts using their email addresses.

In addition to the three main login types, you can also import classes from either Google Classroom or Clever, if your district uses those tools.

You can complete the rest of the section setup however you like. Because we aren't directly using one of the existing curricula, it doesn't really matter what course you assign to students (though it could hurt to put them in CS Discoveries).

Assigning Work

When assigning students the projects from this book, the easiest approach is to have them remix the app templates I've provided online (**creativecodingbook.com**). You can ask them to manually remix by viewing code and then clicking Remix, or you can provide a link that automatically remixes by adding "/remix" to the end of the project URL you share (replacing "/edit" or "/view" if necessary). Alternatively, you can send students directly to the Code.org website (**studio.code.org/projects/applab**) to start a new project with a blank slate.

Collecting Work

Though working outside of the existing curricula means we can't use all features of the Code.org teacher dashboard, there is one feature that will be immensely useful. When viewing your section details, the Projects tab will take you to a view of *all* projects created by students assigned to your section. To make life a bit easier, I like to enforce a strict project-naming scheme so I know when a project is ready for me to review. For example, you might have students name their projects

"Project: Text Adventure [In Progress]" while it's being worked on, and "Project: Text Adventure [Submitted]" when it's ready for review.

This is just the bare minimum needed to get set up on the Code.org platform. If you want to dig deeper into some of the classroom management tools, you can find lots of tutorials at in the support section (**support.code.org**).

Considerations for Other Languages

I designed all of the projects around App Lab for the simplicity of sticking with a single language and environment. App Lab a great multipurpose programming environment that allows students to transition from blocks to text at their own pace. It's not, however, the only tool you can use to implement these projects, nor is it the right tool for every kind of programming project or classroom. Here are some modifications to each project that you might make for a handful of other popular programming tools for middle school.

Scratch

Scratch is a programming language and environment all wrapped up in one. Developed by the Lifelong Kindergarten group at MIT, Scratch is designed to reflect Seymore Paperts' goals of a "low floor," "wide walls," and a "high ceiling." Scratch's block-based environment allow students to explore and discover functionality on their own, and its combination of multiple programming paradigms means that you can tackle any given problem in a lot of different ways.

When modifying any of these programs for use in Scratch, the biggest difference you'll need to deal with is the transition from screens and elements to stages and sprites. Scratch's central thinking tool is the sprite—a character on the screen that students interact with through code. Just about anything you create using design elements in App Lab will be replaced by a sprite in Scratch. Button to click? Sprite! Paragraph of text? Sprite! Multiple screens? Multiple sprites! If you're interested in learning more about how to program in Scratch, check out the tips and tutorials online (**scratch.mit.edu/tips**).

Examples of each project created in Scratch can be found on this book's website (**creativecodingbook.com/scratch**).

The basic modifications that need to be made are as follows.

ELA

Scratch doesn't have the same concept of screens and events that we used in App Lab. Instead you would use sprites and costumes to replicate a similar tool. Create one sprite that represents the text area of the screen. For each screen that we designed for App Lab, you'll create a costume for your sprite that contains that same text.

SOCIAL STUDIES

The flexibility of this project makes it relatively simple to modify for Scratch. The biggest change is that you'll use backgrounds and/or sprites instead of screens and design elements. Scratch in general is less effective at text-based apps, so you'll need to point students toward the text tool in the sprite costume editor to create sprite costumes that contain your text.

MATH

Scratch doesn't allow for the same kind of functional programming that we used in App Lab, so to create a similar kind of app, we won't be able to use algebraic functions (ones which return values and behave without side effects). Instead, we'll need to rely on procedural programming to achieve a similar result. We can use the ask and wait block to take the input number(s), use the math and answer blocks to calculate a result, and display the result using say.

SCIENCE

While Scratch doesn't support the same kind of database backend that we used in App Lab, it does include "cloud" variables that can persist across multiple uses of the same program. Using cloud variables to store experiment is a bit more constraining than using a full table, so you'll need to design an experiment that only requires incrementing a value.

Python

Python is commonly used as a first text-based programming language in middle school. Unlike JavaScript, or other popular C-like languages, Python relies on a syntax that attempts to be more human readable. Instead of curly braces (e.g., {}) and semicolons to structure code, Python relies primarily on white space. For example, let's compare the same loop written in JavaScript and Python:

Javascript

```javascript
for (var i=0; i<10; i++) {
  console.log(i);
}
```

Python

```python
for number in range(0, 10):
  print(number)
```

Notice that the Python code, when read aloud, sounds fairly close to regular English. This allows the code to better communicate meaning without additional syntactical elements. If you're considering using Python in the classroom, it's important to recognize that Python, like JavaScript, is just a language. App Lab provides a lot of additional features that make programming in JavaScript easier. To replicate these projects in Python, you'll need to install a development environment and some additional libraries. Building graphical apps requires much more work, so I'd recommend that unless you want to invest a lot more time teaching Python, you'll want to focus solely on text-based programs. An up-to-date selection of both environments and libraries, along with example code for each project, can be found on this book's website (**creativecodingbook.com/python**).

ELA

Python is a fantastic language for processing text, which makes this project a natural fit. By using only the text console, this project feels even more like Zork and other text-based adventures from the 1980s.

SOCIAL STUDIES

Python on it's own isn't nearly as easy to make a standalone app with as App Lab. The online example uses a relatively lightweight Python framework called Flask to build the app, but even still, I probably wouldn't recommend this unless you're really invested in using Python.

MATH

If you can live without a pretty, graphical interface, this project works really well in Python. Define all of your functions in a Python file, import the file, and run the functions from the command line.

SCIENCE

Python is the go-to language for scientists in lots of fields, and it's a fantastic tool for processing and manipulating data. The challenge here is connecting it up to a database that can store experiment data. There a are a few ways to approach this, depending on your goals. If it's not important that the data persists (meaning that it doesn't really matter if all of your data is lost when you stop the program) then you can use simple variables to store collected experiment data. If persistent data is important, there are a number of different approaches to setting up a quick database, including the python packages "tinydb" and "sqlite3."

ISTE Standards for Students

The ISTE Standards for Students emphasize the skills and qualities we want for students, enabling them to engage and thrive in a connected, digital world. The standards are designed for use by educators across the curriculum, with every age student, with a goal of cultivating these skills throughout a student's academic career. Both students and teachers will be responsible for achieving foundational technology skills to fully apply the standards. The reward, however, will be educators who skillfully mentor and inspire students to amplify learning with technology and challenge them to be agents of their own learning.

1. **Empowered Learner**

   Students leverage technology to take an active role in choosing, achieving and demonstrating competency in their learning goals, informed by the learning sciences. Students:

   a. articulate and set personal learning goals, develop strategies leveraging technology to achieve them and reflect on the learning process itself to improve learning outcomes.

   b. build networks and customize their learning environments in ways that support the learning process.

   c. use technology to seek feedback that informs and improves their practice and to demonstrate their learning in a variety of ways.

   d. understand the fundamental concepts of technology operations, demonstrate the ability to choose, use and troubleshoot current technologies and are able to transfer their knowledge to explore emerging technologies.

2. **Digital Citizen**

   Students recognize the rights, responsibilities and opportunities of living, learning and working in an interconnected digital world, and they act and model in ways that are safe, legal and ethical. Students:

a. cultivate and manage their digital identity and reputation and are aware of the permanence of their actions in the digital world.

b. engage in positive, safe, legal and ethical behavior when using technology, including social interactions online or when using networked devices.

c. demonstrate an understanding of and respect for the rights and obligations of using and sharing intellectual property.

d. manage their personal data to maintain digital privacy and security and are aware of data-collection technology used to track their navigation online.

3. Knowledge Constructor

Students critically curate a variety of resources using digital tools to construct knowledge, produce creative artifacts and make meaningful learning experiences for themselves and others. Students:

a. plan and employ effective research strategies to locate information and other resources for their intellectual or creative pursuits.

b. evaluate the accuracy, perspective, credibility and relevance of information, media, data or other resources.

c. curate information from digital resources using a variety of tools and methods to create collections of artifacts that demonstrate meaningful connections or conclusions.

d. build knowledge by actively exploring real-world issues and problems, developing ideas and theories and pursuing answers and solutions.

4. Innovative Designer

Students use a variety of technologies within a design process to identify and solve problems by creating new, useful or imaginative solutions. Students:

a. know and use a deliberate design process for generating ideas, testing theories, creating innovative artifacts or solving authentic problems.

b. select and use digital tools to plan and manage a design process that considers design constraints and calculated risks.

c. develop, test and refine prototypes as part of a cyclical design process.

d. exhibit a tolerance for ambiguity, perseverance and the capacity to work with open-ended problems.

5. Computational Thinker

Students develop and employ strategies for understanding and solving problems in ways that leverage the power of technological methods to develop and test solutions. Students:

a. formulate problem definitions suited for technology-assisted methods such as data analysis, abstract models and algorithmic thinking in exploring and finding solutions.

b. collect data or identify relevant data sets, use digital tools to analyze them, and represent data in various ways to facilitate problem-solving and decision-making.

c. break problems into component parts, extract key information, and develop descriptive models to understand complex systems or facilitate problem-solving.

d. understand how automation works and use algorithmic thinking to develop a sequence of steps to create and test automated solutions.

6. Creative Communicator

Students communicate clearly and express themselves creatively for a variety of purposes using the platforms, tools, styles, formats and digital media appropriate to their goals. Students:

a. choose the appropriate platforms and tools for meeting the desired objectives of their creation or communication.

b. create original works or responsibly repurpose or remix digital resources into new creations.

c. communicate complex ideas clearly and effectively by creating or using a variety of digital objects such as visualizations, models or simulations.

d. publish or present content that customizes the message and medium for their intended audiences.

7. Global Collaborator

Students use digital tools to broaden their perspectives and enrich their learning by collaborating with others and working effectively in teams locally and globally. Students:

a. use digital tools to connect with learners from a variety of backgrounds and cultures, engaging with them in ways that broaden mutual understanding and learning.

b. use collaborative technologies to work with others, including peers, experts or community members, to examine issues and problems from multiple viewpoints.

c. contribute constructively to project teams, assuming various roles and responsibilities to work effectively toward a common goal.

d. explore local and global issues and use collaborative technologies to work with others to investigate solutions.

Your opinion matters: Tell us how we're doing!

Your feedback helps ISTE create the best possible resources for teaching and learning in the digital age. Share your thoughts with the community or tell us how we're doing!

You can:

- Write a review at amazon.com or barnesandnoble.com.

- Mention this book on social media and follow ISTE on Twitter @iste, Facebook @ISTEconnects or Instagram @isteconnects

Email us at books@iste.org with your questions or comments.